SUSHI

COOKBOOK

FOR BEGINNERS

*Over 100 delicious sushi
Recipes Make Sushi at Home
step by step.*

Jose M Coley

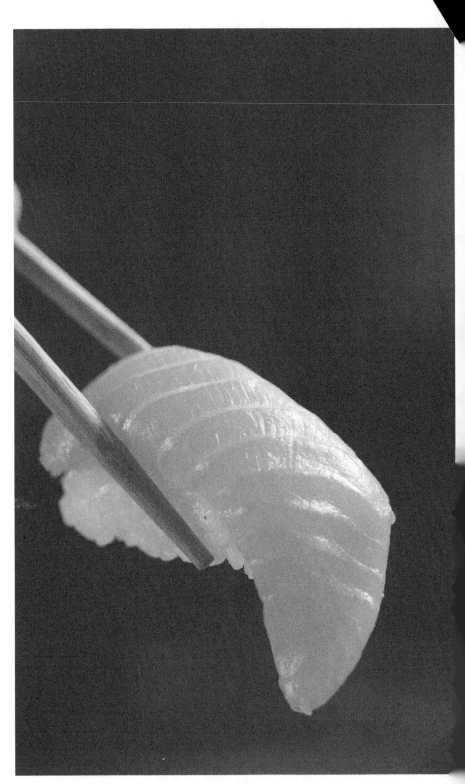

Table of Contents

5

INTRODUCTION
Everything You Need to Know About Japanese Cuisine

Sushi has a long and illustrious history, and one of the most remarkable aspects of this history is that sushi is always developing. Sushi, which was first described in China during the second century, was initially developed as a method of food preservation. Fish was put in rice and left to ferment, which allowed the fish to remain edible for an extended period. The rice was subsequently thrown away, and the fish was consumed as and when it was necessary.

Throughout China, the practice gained popularity, and by the seventh century, it had found its way to Japan, where seafood has long been a staple dish. The Japanese made a modest modification to the method by electing to consume the rice along with the fish instead of separately. Rice had been seasoned by the 17th century, transforming what had originally been a salvific procedure into a well enjoyed delicacy. Matsumoto Yoshi chi of Edo (now Tokyo) pioneered the production of instant sushi,' which is considered the origin of modern-day sushi.

Modern sushi

A guy by the name of Hanaya Yohei envisioned a major shift in the way sushi was made and given to the public in the early nineteenth century. Instead of wrapping the fish in rice, he placed a piece of fish on top of an oblong-shaped piece of seasoned rice, which he then wrapped around the fish. As a result of this form of sushi, it is now known as either 'nigiri sushi,' or simply 'edomae sushi,' and it is one of the most popular ways to consume sushi not just in Japan, but also across the rest of the globe.

Anaya Yoshie and other sushi chefs marketed this innovative new type of sushi from street booths all around the city and surrounding areas. Even though the booths were extremely popular with the bustling Japanese culture prior to World War II, the stalls were forced to close and relocate indoors, where it was deemed more sanitary, after the war.

It is a worldwide phenomenon.

During the late 1970s, Japanese firms began expanding into the United States, and an increasing number of sushi restaurants sprang up to cater to the Japanese businessmen who were based in the area. It was often regarded as a "Japanese twist on fast food," and while it was first intended as a short snack, it swiftly evolved into a full-fledged dining experience for those unfamiliar with the concept.
Without a question, Sushi had piqued the curiosity of many Americans, but many were hesitant to eat raw fish because of the dangers associated with it. The California Roll was established as a method to gradually introduce folks who were unfamiliar with sushi — it is the ideal starter piece of sushi. Sushi was a huge popularity, and as more and more Westerners began to consume sushi, Edo-style sushi began to mingle with western culture.

What to expect in the new year?

For the purposes of this article, sushi is defined as any food that is created using vinegared sushi rice. It is a popular misconception that the name sushi refers to "raw fish," however this is not the case. Sushi is a Japanese word that literally translates as "it's sour," alluding to the sour flavor of vinegared rice. Aside from that, certain varieties of sushi do not include any fish at all, such as our Vegetarian Roll, which is stuffed with poached asparagus, cucumber, caramelized miso wild mushrooms, and burdock root, and then stacked with avocado and drizzled with sweet black miso aioli to finish.

In Australia and across the world, sushi may be found in a wide variety of flavors and textures.

Makizushi

Makizushi is Japanese for "rolled sushi." If anything is wrapped in Nori (seaweed), it is commonly considered to be a sushi roll, although it can also be wrapped in other materials such as a thin omelette, soy paper, cucumber, or shiso (perilla) leaves. Among the many variations on rolled sushi are:

Hosomaki is a thin roll filled with rice on the inside and nori on the outside.

Chumak is a medium-sized roll with rice on the interior and nori on the outside.

Futomaki - a thick roll with rice on the interior and nori on the exterior – is an appetizer.

Uramaki is made of rice on the exterior and nori on the interior.

Temaki is a hand-rolled or cone-shaped Japanese pastry.

Sushi Nigiri (Nigiri Sushi)

Nigiri sushi literally translates as "hand-pressed sushi." An oblong of rice, usually hand-molded, is served with a swipe of wasabi on top, and a topping of salmon or tuna completes the dish, which is traditionally served cold.

Chirashizushi

Chirashizushi is a Japanese term that means "scattered sushi." Traditionally, it is served in a bowl with sushi rice, and it is frequently topped with nine different types of ingredients. It is popular in Japanese households due to the fact that it is simple to prepare.

Inarizushi

Inarizushi, which literally translates as "carrying rice," is a pouch of fried tofu (abura age) that is filled with sushi rice. It is made by slicing tofu into thin slices and deep-frying them at temperatures ranging from 110 to 120 degrees Celsius, followed by 180-200 degrees Celsius.

Oshizushi

Oshizushi is Japanese for "pressed sushi," and it is produced by pressing raw fish into a wooden mold. After that, it is sliced into squares or rectangles before being served.
Sushi preparation and consumption

1. Get rid of the dunk

Picking up a piece of sushi and immediately drenching it with soy sauce is one of the most common blunders individuals do while preparing sushi. The soy is subsequently absorbed by the rice, leaving you with only a faint flavor of soy sauce. The soy sauce is intended to enhance the flavor of the sushi vinegar rather than to disguise it. Instead of dipping the sushi in the soy sauce, consider tilting the sushi towards the soy sauce and eating it in one mouthful.

2. Keep wasabi in a separate container.

Although many Westerners are in the habit of incorporating wasabi into their meal of soy sauce, this dilutes the potency of the wasabi. As an alternative, dab a tiny bit of wasabi straight onto your sushi before delicately dipping it in the soy sauce, allowing each separate flavor to meld together on your tongue.

3. Pay attention to the sequence

If you find yourself in front of a beautiful sushi platter, resist the temptation to reach out and take the first roll you see. Take a more gradual approach, beginning with sashimi and lighter fish such as snapper or King George whiting before progressing to richer flavors such as salmon and kingfish. After that, you may top it off with some delectable tuna. Don't forget to eat the pickled ginger in between mouthfuls!

4. Make use of chopsticks

You could feel self-conscious at first, but if you don't put in the effort, you'll never become better. Apart than that, it's tradition!

5. Take pleasure in the experience

As a dining experience rather than something that can be produced at home or purchased as takeaway, modern sushi is intended to be savored. To get the most out of sushi, start by visiting a reputed Japanese restaurant and then following the guidelines outlined above.

Recipes

HAMBURGER HELPER SUSHI ROLLS

Prep: 45 MIN Total: 4 HR 0 MIN

Ingredients

- 1 box Betty Crocker™ Hamburger Helper™ cheeseburger macaroni
- 1 lb ground beef
- ¾ cup of water (less than package instructions)
- 2 cups of milk
- 1 tsp unflavored gelatin
- 1 package Food Should Taste Good™ original sweet potato chips.
- 15 green beans

Instructions

1. Green beans can be blanched by heating them in salted boiling water for about 5 minutes, straining, and then submerging them in cold water for a few seconds.
2. Use just 3/4 cup of water when making Hamburger Helpers according to the package instructions. Gently remove the pan from heat and mix in the gelatin.
3. Refrigerate for about one hour before serving.
4. Keep the Hamburger Helpers from drying out by covering it with plastic wrap. Make sure you repeat this technique at least twice or three times for the best results. Green beans should be placed in the center of the tortilla before it is rolled up.
5. Twist the ends together to make a log that is perfectly spherical.
6. Two hours in the freezer should do the trick.
7. Crushed sweet potato chips can be used to coat the round.
8. Make 1-inch circles and place on a baking sheet. Bake at the lowest temperature for about 15 minutes, or until the meat is no longer pink.
9. The rolls should be served with sriracha when they are slightly warmer than room temperature. You don't want to overheat the rolls, or they'll crumble.

15

TEMAKI SUSHI – EASY HAND ROLLED SUSHI

Prep Time:5 minutes Cook Time:0 minutes. Total Time:5 minutes

Ingredients

For the rice:
- 6 cups cooked sushi rice this equals 2 cups of uncooked sushi rice if you need to cook a fresh batch.
- 2 tbsp sushi vinegar Sub with 1½ tbsp rice wine vinegar, 1 tsp sugar and a pinch of salt

For the wrapper:
- 2 nori sheets per person, sliced in half.

For the fillings:
- • 200 g tuna canned, in brine.
- 2-3 tbsp kewpie mayonnaise
- 1 carrot finely sliced.
- 1 cucumber sliced into strips.

For dipping:
- soy sauce
- wasabi

Instructions

1. Move the finished sushi rice to a shallow, broad pan or plate.

2. Once the rice has finished cooking, add the sushi vinegar, and gently mix it in with a flat rice paddle so that you don't break up the grains. Before serving, the rice should be allowed to cool fully.

3. In a small bowl, thoroughly blend the tuna and kewpie mayo. You may always add additional kewpie mayo to get the desired creamy consistency and rich flavor.

4. Raise a sheet of nori (which you've cut in half or into a rectangle) and hold it in your palm or set it down on a plate. Put a triangle mound of rice in the upper left corner.

5. Spread on your preferred toppings (such as the tuna with kewpie mayo, carrot, and cucumber). Roll the dough into a cone shape, folding the bottom left corner up and over the contents.

LOBSTER HAWAIIAN SUSHI ROLLS

Prep time: 1 hours Cook time: 20 minutes.

Ingredients

- 2 sheets of nori
- 2 cups of cooked sushi rice
- 1 tbsp toasted sesame seeds (I like a blend of white and black)
- 2 (6-ounce) lobster tails, removed from shells, cut into 1/2-inch-thick pieces
- 1 ripe mango, pitted, peeled, sliced into thin strips.
- 1/2 of 1 English cucumber, quartered, cored, and julienned.
- 1 ripe avocado, peeled, pitted, and sliced into thin strips.
- Wasabi
- Soy sauce

Instructions

1. Using plastic wrap, cover a sushi mat made of bamboo. To create a sushi mat, layout the nori sheet. Over the nori, spread a uniform layer of sushi rice.

2. Add sesame seeds to the rice before serving. Make sure the nori is facing up by carefully flipping it over. Place the cooked lobster in the middle of the nori, as described above.

3. Add mango, avocado, and cucumber. Roll up firmly, giving a few gentle squeezes as you do, starting at one long end and using the bamboo mat as a help. Sushi should be cut into eight pieces. Make a second batch with the remaining ingredients.

SMOKY SPICED CARROT RICE

Under 30 minutes

Ingredients

- 1 bunch carrot peeled and sliced.
- 1 tbsp cooking oil of preference, or water
- ½ white onion, diced
- ½ tsp salt
- ½ tsp pepper
- ½ tsp garlic powder
- 1 tsp smoked paprika.
- fresh parsley, for garnish

Instructions

1. Process the carrots until they resemble "rice" in texture in a food processor.
2. Overheat, add the olive oil, then the onions and sauté until they begin to turn translucent.
3. Then add the carrots and rice and simmer until the rice is cooked. Stir periodically.
4. Parsley is a good garnish.
5. Enjoy!

CUCUMBER-AVOCADO CAULIFLOWER RICE SUSHI

Active:35 mins Total:35 mins

Ingredients

- 8 sheets nori
- 4 cups of cooked cauliflower rice, at room temperature, divided.
- 2 avocados, sliced, divided.
- 1 cup of cucumber matchsticks, divided.
- 8 tbsp Sriracha mayo, divided.

Instructions

1. Bamboo rolling mats may be used to roll out nori sheets. Use your hands to spread and press half a cup of cauliflower rice onto the sheet.
2. Place 1/8 of the avocado slices and 1/8 of the cucumber matchsticks approximately 1 inch from the bottom of the rice in a vase or other serving vessel.
3. The last inch of the nori should be left unwrapped. Finish rolling the sushi by dipping your fingers into a basin of water and wetting the exposed nori.
4. Assemble the cylinder by rolling a bamboo mat over a sushi mat. Slice into eight pieces. Mix the Sriracha mayo with 1 tbsp of water.
5. For each additional item, do Steps 2 through 4.

VEGGIE SUSHI

Active:35 mins Total:35 mins

Ingredients

- 2 ½ tbsp rice vinegar
- 1 tbsp sugar
- ¾ tsp salt
- 3 cups of sushi rice (600 g), cooked.
- 1 cup of black rice (230 g), cooked.
- 4 sheets roasted nori.
- SHIITAKE VEGGIE ROLL
- 1 tbsp sesame oil
- 1 cup of shiitake mushroom (75 g), sliced.
- 1 tbsp soy sauce
- ¼ tsp garlic powder
- pepper, as need
- 8 leaves fresh spinach.
- 4 sticks cucumber
- 4 sticks carrot
- vegetable oil, for frying
- ½ cup of all-purpose

Instructions

1. Salt and sugar are added to a small saucepan over medium-high heat and whisked together. Until the salt and sugar are completely dissolved, bring to a boil, stirring constantly. It's time to remove it.

2. In a large bowl, combine the cooked sushi rice with a second medium bowl of the cooked black rice and mix thoroughly. Incorporate 34 of the rice vinegar mixture into the sushi rice, while the remaining 14 is added to the banned rice. Add the vinegar mixture and whisk until it is evenly dispersed.

3. Make the shiitake vegetable bun by following these instructions: Add the sesame oil to a medium saucepan and bring it to a boil. Adding the shiitakes and garlic powder and pepper while the oil is heating, cook for 6-8 minutes before the mushrooms release their juices and begin to crisp up.

4. Place a single sheet of nori on a sushi mat made of bamboo. On top of the nori, place 1 cup of sushi rice (230 g). To keep your fingers from becoming sticky when handling the rice, prepare a small dish of water. Make a 1-inch

- flour (60 g)
- 1 tsp baking powder
- ½ tsp salt
- ¼ tsp pepper
- ¾ cup of ice water (180 mL)
- 1 medium sweet potato, cut into sticks.
- 2 slices avocado
- AVOCADO CUCUMBER MANGO ROLL
- 4 slices avocado
- 4 sticks cucumber
- 4 sticks mango
- TERIYAKI TOFU ROLL
- 4 strips teriyaki tofu, baked.
- 4 sticks red bell pepper
- 4 sticks carrot
- FOR SERVING
- wasabi
- pickled ginger
- soy sauce

(2-cm) border at the top of the roll by spreading the rice evenly over it.

5. Layer the spinach, cucumber, carrot, and shiitake mushrooms on the bottom quarter of the nori. While rolling the nori, keep the veggies in place with your fingers. To make a tight sushi roll, squeeze the bamboo mat around the roll as you proceed. To make eight pieces of sushi, cut the sushi roll in half and then quarters.

6. A medium saucepan of vegetable oil should reach 375 degrees Fahrenheit (190 degrees Celsius).

7. Stir the flour, baking powder, salt, and pepper in a medium bowl with a fork and mix thoroughly. Using an immersion blender, mix in the ice water until it is completely dissolved. With your fingers, toss the sweet potato sticks in the batter to coat them well.

8. As many as you can fit on one piece of a spider and delicately put it into the deep-fried sweet potato. Transfer to a paper towel-lined dish and continue cooking for another 3-4 minutes, until crispy.

9. Place a single sheet of nori on a sushi mat made of bamboo. On top of the nori, place 1 cup of sushi rice (230 g). Make a 1-inch (2-cm) border at the top of the roll by spreading the rice evenly over it.

10. Sweet potato tempura and avocado should be layered on the nori's bottom quarter. While rolling the nori, keep the veggies in place with your fingers. To achieve a tight sushi roll, squeeze

the bamboo mat around the sushi roll as you proceed. To make eight pieces of sushi, cut the sushi roll in half and then quarters.

11. Place a nori sheet on a bamboo sushi mat, followed by an avocado, cucumber, and mango filling. On top of the nori, place a dollop of prohibited rice. Make a 1-inch (2-cm) border at the top of the roll by spreading the rice evenly over it.

12. A quarter of a nori sheet should be layered with avocados, cucumbers, and mangoes. While rolling the nori, keep the filling in place with your fingertips. To achieve a tight sushi roll, squeeze the bamboo mat around the sushi roll as you proceed. To make eight pieces of sushi, cut the sushi roll in half and then quarters.

13. Nori is placed on a bamboo sushi mat, then a layer of teriyaki tofu is placed on top of it. On top of the nori, add the remaining two cups of sushi rice. Make a 1-inch (2-cm) border at the top of the roll by spreading the rice evenly over it.

14. Layer the teriyaki tofu, red bell pepper, and carrot on the bottom quarter of the roll. While rolling the nori, keep the filling in place with your fingertips. To achieve a tight sushi roll, squeeze the bamboo mat around the sushi roll as you proceed. To make eight pieces of sushi, cut the sushi roll in half and then quarters.

15. Wasabi, pickled ginger, and soy sauce should accompany the sushi.

16. Enjoy!

SWEET HEAT SALMON

Active:45 mins Total:45 mins

Ingredients

- 2 cups of rice rinsed and drained.
- 2 cups of water
- 1/4 cup of rice vinegar
- 2 tbsp sugar
- 1/2 tsp salt
- 7 fresh asparagus spears, trimmed.
- Bamboo sushi mat
- 7 nori sheets
- 1 small cucumber, julienned.
- 1 small carrot, julienned.
- 2 jalapeno peppers seeded and julienned.
- 1 medium ripe avocado, peeled.
- 1/4 cup of julienned daikon radish
- Reduced-sodium soy sauce and prepared wasabi.

Instructions

1. In a medium saucepan, combine the pureed preserves, water, jalapenos, and garlic. Over medium heat, bring to a boil. Cook for 15 minutes, stirring often, before reduced by half. To thicken the sauce, add tamari (or soy sauce) and vinegar and cook for another 4 to 8 minutes. Take off the heat. A tablespoon of lemon or lime juice should be added.

2. Prepare grill or broiler to medium-high to high heat while this is all going on. Salt and oil the fish before cooking.

3. The grill rack should be sprayed with cooking spray, or the salmon could be placed on a rimmed baking sheet. In a grill or broiler, cook the salmon skin-side down for 10 to 15 minutes, depending on thickness. The salmon should be transferred to a serving tray using two big spatulas. Apply the warm glaze on top.

4. Serve with remaining 1 tablespoon lemon (or lime) juice and arugula/radishes/mint/chervil dressing. Add extra jalapeno slices or lemon wedges if preferred to the fish and salad.

VEGGIE SUSHI ROLLS

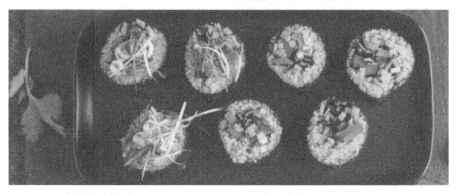

Total Time Prep: 1 hour

Ingredients

- ¾ cup of fruit preserves, such as blackberry or peach, pureed
- 6 tbsp water
- 1 jalapeño pepper, thinly sliced, +more for garnish.
- 2 cloves garlic, chopped.
- ¼ cup of white-wine or cider vinegar
- 1 ½ tbsp reduced sodium tamari
- 2 tbsp lemon or lime juice, divided.
- 1 ½ pounds skin-on salmon fillet
- 1 tbsp extra-virgin olive oil
- ¼ tsp kosher salt
- 3 cups of packed arugula
- 1 cup of thinly sliced radishes

Instructions

1. In a medium saucepan, combine the pureed preserves, water, jalapenos, and garlic. Over medium heat, bring to a boil. Cook for 15 minutes, stirring often, before reduced by half. To thicken the sauce, add tamari (or soy sauce) and vinegar and cook for another 4 to 8 minutes. Take off the heat. A tablespoon of lemon or lime juice should be added.

2. Prepare grill or broiler to medium-high to high heat while this is all going on. Salt and oil the fish before cooking.

3. The grill rack should be sprayed with cooking spray, or the salmon could be placed on a rimmed baking sheet. In a grill or broiler, cook the salmon skin-side down for 10 to 15 minutes, depending on thickness. The salmon should be transferred to a serving tray using two big spatulas. Apply the warm glaze on top.

4. Serve with remaining 1 tablespoon lemon (or lime) juice and arugula/radishes/mint/chervil dressing. Add extra jalapeno slices or lemon wedges if preferred to the fish and salad.

- ¼ cup of fresh mint or chervil leaves, torn
- Lemon wedges for garnish

SPICY TUNA HAND ROLLS

Active:45 mins Total:45 mins

Ingredients	Instructions

For the rice:

- 1 1/4 cups of sushi rice, rinsed.
- 1 tbsp rice vinegar (unseasoned)
- 1 tbsp sugar
- Kosher salt
- 2 tbsp sesame seeds, toasted.
- For the sauce:
- 2/3 cup of mayonnaise
- 2 tbsp fresh lemon juice
- 3 to 4 tsp Sriracha (Asian Chile sauce)
- 1 tbsp soy sauce
- 1 tsp sesame oil
- 1 tsp grated peeled ginger.

1. Prepare the rice by mixing it with 1 1/4 cups water in a small saucepan. After a few minutes of boiling, cover and soak for 15 minutes. After removing from the heat, cover and set aside for 10 minutes. Meanwhile, in a large pot, mix together the rice vinegar, sugar, and 1 teaspoon of salt. With a rubber spatula, mix in the sesame seeds and cooled rice until they are evenly distributed. If making the rice ahead of time, it may be stored in the refrigerator for up to 2 hours under a wet towel.

2. Mix mayonnaise with lemon juice and Sriracha; add soy sauce and sesame oil; then add ginger. Frigate until ready to use, then cover and chill.

3. It's time for the tuna! Salt and pepper the tuna to taste. Heat a nonstick skillet over medium-high heat. 2 minutes each side in the vegetable oil. Refrigerate for up to an hour or until ready to use. Transfer to a plate.

For the tuna and rolls:

- 3/4-pound ahi tuna
- Kosher salt and freshly ground pepper
- 1 tbsp vegetable oil
- 6 sheets seaweed
- 1 avocado, pitted, peeled, and thinly sliced.
- 1 cucumber
- 1 carrot
- 1/2 bunch chives
- Pickled ginger, for serving.

4. Put the rolls together: Use a medium-hot gas or electric burner to gently toast the seaweed. Cut each sheet in half with shears to produce 12 rectangles. Salt and pepper the tuna before slicing it into cubes. The long side of a seaweed rectangle should face you. Using wet fingertips, apply rice to the left side of the sheet, leaving a 1-inch border. Add a tablespoon of sauce, a slice of tuna, a piece of avocado, and a few pieces of cucumber, carrot, and chives. Roll the seaweed firmly into a cone shape from the bottom left corner, moistening the edge of the seaweed to seal it. For each additional item, do Steps 2 through 4. Serve with more sauce and pickled ginger.

SPICY BEEF SUSHI BOWL

Prep: 45 min Cook: 25 min

Ingredients

-
- Sushi Rice
- 2 cups of cooked short-grain rice, find in the Asian section.
- 1/4 cups of rice vinegar, find in the Asian section.
- 2 tbsp sugar
- 1/2 tsp salt
- Spicy Beef Seasoning
- 2 tbsp fish sauce, find in the Asian section.
- 2–3 tbsp Chile-garlic sauce or Sriracha
- 2 tbsp soy sauce
- 2 tbsp rice vinegar
- 1 tbsp water
- 1 tbsp fresh ginger, minced.
- Spicy Beef
- 1-pound ground beef
- 2 tsp toasted sesame oil
- Spicy Beef Sushi Bowl Dressing

Instructions

1. Using the package guidelines, prepare 2 cups of rice for sushi-style dishes. Typically, 1 cup of uncooked rice serves this purpose. 2 cups of cooked rice = 1 cup of water.

2. Mix the sushi dressing ingredients while rice is frying. a Pyrex measuring cup or glass bowl works well for this. Stir after 15 seconds of microwave cooking at 50% power. Remove from consideration. Alternatively, you may cook it on a stovetop at a low heat. The objective is to melt the sugar.

3. Cooked rice may be spread out on a big baking sheet using a wooden spoon using this method. Gently mix the dressing into the hot rice with a wooden spoon (warm rice absorbs the dressing better), then pour it over the top and serve right away. Add rice to a large bowl and mix thoroughly. A damp cloth or paper towel can be used to keep the rice moist until it's time to cook. The sticky nature of this rice can be mitigated by putting your hands in a bowl of cold water before handling it.

4. It is possible to make this a day or two in advance.

5. Seasoning for Beef Make a mixture of the

27

- 2 ½ tbsp rice vinegar
- 2 tbsp fish sauce
- 2 tbsp water
- 1 tbsp sugar
- Toppings
- 1 tbsp toasted sesame seeds
- 1 cup of cucumber, diced.
- ½ red pepper, diced
- ½ to 1 jalapeno, minced
- ½ cup of fresh herbs (basil, cilantro, parsley), torn into pieces

sauces listed above except for the fish sauce.

6. Beef with a Kick of Heat Add oil and ground beef to a large pan set over medium heat. After breaking up the meat with a spoon or spatula, spread it evenly in a single layer. Wait until the bottom is crispy and browned, about 4 minutes. Flip the meat over. Cook for a total of 4-5 minutes before serving. You're looking for beef that's been charred to a crisp. Drain the fat. Toss in the Spicy Beef Seasoning (Chile-garlic combination), decrease the heat, and simmer for about 3 to 5 minutes.

7. Preparation of a Spicy Beef Sushi Bowl Dressing. Warm the rice vinegar, fish sauce, water, and sugar while the beef is cooking. Because the sugar must be melted, you may require an additional ten seconds of cooking time. Remove from consideration.

8. It just takes a few minutes for the sesame seeds to burst and begin to smell toasted in a pan set to medium-low heat.

9. assemble the dish: in a bowl, layer sushi rice with spicy beef and fresh herbs; garnish with red pepper and jalapeño. Sauced Sushi Bowl Dressing on top. If desired, top with sesame seeds.

FUTOMAKI THICK SUSHI ROLLS FILLED WITH VEGETABLES

Cook Time: 30 minutes.

Ingredients

- 5 Sushi Rolls
- ⬜Sushi Rice⬜
- 2 cups of rice
- 5 g kombu (kelp)
- 20 cc cooking's sake
- 340 cc water
- ⬜Sushi Vinegar⬜
- 4 Tbsp rice vinegar
- 3 Tbsp sugar
- 1 tsp salt
- ⬜Tamagoyaki - Rolled Egg Omelets⬜
- 3 eggs
- 2 tsp sugar
- 1 tsp mirin (sweet sake)
- 3 tsp cooking's sake
- dash salt
- ⬜Simmered Shiitake Mushroom⬜
- 5 dried shiitake mushrooms, rehydrated in 1 cup of water ⬜keep the 100cc water for

Instructions

1. Using the package guidelines, prepare 2 cups of rice for sushi-style dishes. Typically, 1 cup of uncooked rice serves this purpose. 2 cups of cooked rice = 1 cup of water.

2. Mix the sushi dressing ingredients while rice is frying. a Pyrex measuring cup or glass bowl works well for this. Stir after 15 seconds of microwave cooking at 50% power. Remove from consideration. Alternatively, you may cook it on a stovetop at a low heat. The objective is to melt the sugar.

3. Cooked rice may be spread out on a big baking sheet using a wooden spoon using this method. Gently mix the dressing into the hot rice with a wooden spoon (warm rice absorbs the dressing better), then pour it over the top and serve right away. Add rice to a large bowl and mix thoroughly. A damp cloth or paper towel can be used to keep the rice moist until it's time to cook. The sticky nature of this rice can be mitigated by putting your hands in a bowl of cold water before handling it.

4. It is possible to make this a day or two in advance.

5. Seasoning for Beef Make a mixture of the

- cooking.
- 2 tsp sugar
- 2 tsp mirin (sweet sake)
- ⬜Remaining Futomaki Ingredients ⬜
- 1 cucumber
- 30 g smoked salmon
- 5 sheets nori (dried seaweed)
- 100 g tuna
- 1 bunch mitumba (Japanese herbs)

Make the Futomaki Sushi Rolls

1. Then lay one-fifth of sushi rice on top of the nori sheet and wrap the sushi into a log shape.
2. Place the rice, tuna, salmon, shiitake mushroom, egg omelet, cucumber spears, and mitumba horizontally on the bamboo mat.
3. Grab the bamboo mat's bottom edge with your fingers while holding the contents in place.
4. Form a tight cylinder by rolling it up like a big cigar.
5. Remove the bamboo mat from the sushi once it has been covered with the nori roll and pressed firmly. Toss out of the way.
6. Count four futomaki rolls and repeat.
7. Apply a plastic cover to futomaki rolls before cooking.
8. Clean the knife with a wet cloth before slicing the futomaki. Cut the sushi rolled with futomaki.

CRAB AND ASPARAGUS SUSHI WITH PONZU SAUCE

PREP TIME: 5MINS COOK TIME: 30MINS.

Ingredients

- 200g sushi rice
- 2 tbs sushi Seasoning
- 6 asparagus spears, blanched, refreshed.
- 250g fresh crab meat
- 2 tbsp Japanese mayonnaise
- 6 sheets nori
- 1 tbsp wasabi paste.
- PONZU SAUCE
- 1/4 cup of (60ml) lemon juice
- 1/4 cup of (60ml) mirin
- 2 tbs obento rice wine Vinegar
- 1 tbs soy sauce
- 2 tbs bonito flakes

Instructions

1. Simply combine the ingredients in a small saucepan, bring to a boil, and then allow to cool before using. Serve in a serving bowl after it has cooled. apart from

2. Using cold running water, rinse the rice to remove any remaining grit or debris. Using 350 ml of cold water, come to a boil over medium heat, then drop the temperature to low and simmer for 11 minutes. Ten minutes after removing the pan from the heat, cover it and let it sit there. Before serving it as a side dish or appetizer, allow it to cool fully.

3. Set aside 10cm lengths of asparagus. Add mayonnaise and spices to crab meat in a bowl. Set away for later.

4. The rice should be divided into six equal amounts. Nori should be placed shiny side down on a sushi mat and rice sprinkled over it with a 2cm border on the edge that is furthest away from you. Wrap one-sixth of crab mixture, an asparagus spear, and a little quantity of wasabi in rice, then wrap it up, elevating your mat as you go. Press down on the water-sprinkled nori border to seal it.

31

Once you have made six rolls, put them in the fridge until you are ready to serve them. Serve the sushi with the ponzu sauce on the side as a garnish.

VEGAN SUSHI ROLLS WITH ASPARAGUS AND TOFU

Prep : 10 minutes CookTime: 30 minutes. Total Time: 40 minutes

Ingredients

For the Rice

- 2 cups of sushi or jasmine rice (I love using jasmine rice because it has a great flavor.
- 1/4 cup of rice vinegar
- 2 Tbsp white sugar
- 1/2 salt
- For the Tofu
- 1 Tbsp soy sauce
- 1/2 tsp vegan oyster sauce
- 1 nori sheet torn into small pieces.
- 2 cloves minced garlic.
- Veggies
- Thinly sliced carrots, cucumber, mushrooms, and avocado.
- Asparagus stalks

Instructions

1. Set the oven temperature to 400°F.
2. Wash and slice all of the produce.
3. Shred nori, soy sauce, oyster sauce, and garlic into a shallow dish. In a saucepan, add tofu and cover it with a thin layer of sauce. Use the same sauce to marinate the asparagus.
4. Bake marinated tofu and asparagus for 30 to 40 minutes on a baking sheet.
5. Put four cups of water to a boil in a saucepan. Stir in the rice, then cover and cook for a few minutes. It's time to dial down the heat.
6. Add rice vinegar, sugar, and salt to the rice after it's done.
7. Cover a baking dish with moist paper towels and spread out the rice evenly.
8. When the tofu, asparagus, and rice have cooled, place a sheet of nori, shiny side down, on a sushi mat. In order to get a single layer of rice, press down hard on the nori sheet with the rice scoop.
9. Start by placing your vegetables and tofu on the bottom half of the nori roll, and then begin rolling by pressing the sushi mat down and rolling until you come to the finish.

- Nori (seaweed) sheets

10. You can add any items that are protruding from the side of the dish. Make 8 bite-sized pieces by cutting the roll in half and then in half again using a sharp knife.

GUNKAN MAKI

Preparation time:25 mins

Ingredients

- for 4 portion(s)
- 6 x 15 g cooked and seasoned.
- 5 slices of smoked salmon
- 6 x 5 g caviar
- 6 x 3 thin slices of cucumber
- 6 x 3 g cream cheese
- For dipping:
- Kikkoman sushi & sashimi soy sauce

Instructions

1. Form a cylinder out of around 15 g of sushi rice using your fingers and the palm of your hand for each sushi. On top of the sushi, spread some creme fraiche and a slice of smoked salmon. Cucumber and caviar are excellent garnishes.

SPICY MANGO & AVOCADO RICE BOWL

Preparation time: 25 mins

Ingredients

- 2 cups of cooked black forbidden rice, or other grain
- 1 14 oz. package extra firm tofu
- drizzle of olive oil
- drizzle of tamari
- 1 mango, cubed.
- 1 scallion, sliced.
- 1 cup of shredded red cabbage
- a few radishes, thinly sliced.
- ½ cup of chopped cucumber
- 1 avocado pitted and diced.
- lime slices
- handful of chopped cilantros
- coconut peanut sauce:
- ⅓ cup of coconut milk
- 2 tbsp peanut butter
- 2 tsp soy sauce
- 2 tsp lime juice
- 1 tsp sriracha

Instructions

1. Brown rice can be substituted for black rice in the cooking process (I use a rice cooker). one cup of rice to two cups of water is the proper ratio.

2. Prepare a baking sheet by lining it with parchment paper and preheating the oven to 400 degrees Fahrenheit.

3. Slice tofu into cubes and mix with olive oil and tamari before serving. Place on a baking sheet and bake for about 15 minutes, or until the sides are golden brown. About twenty to thirty minutes. Serve with a little sriracha sauce drizzled over the top after it has been removed from the oven.

4. Meanwhile, assemble the sauce ingredients and set aside. A tight-fitting lid is required to keep the mixture from spilling out of the jar. Adjust the seasonings to your liking.

5. Then add mango, cilantro, scallions, and tofu to the bowls you've assembled. Serve with coconut sauce, more sriracha, and lime slices on the side.

SPICY SALMON AND AVOCADO CAULIFLOWER RICE SUSHI ROLL

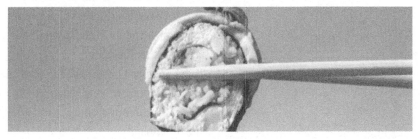

Prep : 15 minutes Cook Time: 5 minutes. Total Time: 20 minutes

Ingredients

Cauliflower Rice:
- 3 cups of grated cauliflower rice
- 2 tbsp rice vinegar
- 2 Tsp tapioca starch
- pinch of salt

Sushi Roll:
- 1/2 lb sushi-grade salmon (or tuna or smoked salmon)
- 1/2 Tbsp Franks Red Hot (if not worried about Whole30/ Paleo, use siracha instead)
- 1 large avocado, sliced.
- 1 cup of cilantro
- 1/2 cucumber
- 3–4 sheets of nori

Dipping Sauce:
- Coco amino and some red pepper flakes
- Spicy Mayo
- 3/4 cup of Compliant

Instructions

1. Grate the cauliflower (I would HIGHLY recommend grating it so that it is the right texture)
2. Cook the grated cauliflower in a pan over medium heat, stirring occasionally.
3. Start stirring the cauliflower with a wooden spoon and let it simmer for a few minutes longer.
4. Rice vinegar and a dash of salt complete the dish.
5. The vinegar should coat the cauliflower in approximately 2 minutes, so keep stirring.
6. The tapioca starch should be added and mixed thoroughly.
7. Remove the rice from the heat and place it in a separate bowl to cool.
8. On a large dish, spread a paper towel.
9. To absorb extra water, lay another paper towel on top of the rice and push down.
10. Return the cauliflower rice to the serving dish.
11. Cut the salmon into cubes and set them in a serving basin.
12. Stir in the Frank's Red Hot or Siracha and keep away until needed.
13. Place the bamboo sushi roller on the cutting board before assembling the sushi roll.

mayo
- 1–2 tbsp Franks Red Hot or Siracha (not Whole30)

14. A nori sheet should be placed on top of it.
15. Using the back of a metal spoon, press down on the cauliflower rice to spread it out and create a thin, compacted layer on the nori.
16. To begin at the bottom of the nori sheet and work your way up away from your body, leave about an inch of the nori sheet exposed.
17. A nori sheet should have a line of cucumbers, cilantro, salmon, and avocado parallel to the bottom, approximately an inch from the bottom.
18. To fold over the fish, etc., raise up the bottom of the nori sheet closest to you, tucking the nori sheet under, and then continue dragging the bamboo roller away from your body while you press down hard on the roll as you go. Then, fold the nori sheet over the salmon, etc.
19. Roll away from you for as long as it takes to accomplish your roll.
20. Use a razor-sharp knife to cut 1-inch slices, cleaning the blade clean after each cut.
21. Serve with coco amines right away.
22. In addition to cilantro, black sesame seeds, and spicy mayonnaise, garnish the dish.

AVOCADO SUSHI

Prep:1 hr Total:1 hrTotal:1 hr

Ingredients

- 2 cups of short-grain white rice, preferably Japonica
- 3-inch piece ginger, peeled
- 1 cup of rice wine vinegar
- 2 tbsp sugar, +1 tsp
- Kosher salt
- 2 mini cucumbers, julienned (1 cup of)
- 2 carrots, peeled and julienned (1 cup of)
- 1/2 tsp sesame oil
- 1/4 cup of mayonnaise
- 1 avocado halved and thinly sliced.
- 1 tbsp toasted sesame seeds
- 6 sheets toasted nori.
- Soy sauce, for serving.

Instructions

1. Rinse the rice many times with clean water, squeezing the rice with your fingertips each time. Prepare remaining ingredients while placing in a strainer set over a basin (at least 20 minutes).

2. Slice the ginger paper-thin down the grain, using a mandolin or a vegetable peeler (for a yield of 1/2 cup). Boil a tiny amount of water, add the ginger, and cook for 5 seconds, draining the water afterward. Reintroduce the saucepan to the heat and mix in the vinegar, sugar, and 3/4 cup water. Salt and pepper to taste. Bring sugar and water to a boil. Reserving half the vinegar mixture, add blanched ginger to the rest of the vinegar to season your rice. Completely cool down.

3. Cook the rice in a small pot with 2 1/2 cups of water. As soon as the mixture reaches a rolling boil, turn down the heat to its lowest setting and cover the pot. Cook the rice in a pot or rice cooker until it is soft and all of the water has been absorbed, approximately 12 minutes, according to the manufacturer's instructions. Remove from the heat. Keep covered for a further 10 minutes. Cook the rice in a large dish for five minutes before serving.

39

Incorporate about one-quarter of the leftover vinegar combination using a broad spatula or plastic bench scraper by fanned-out the rice. Use a kitchen towel to cover the surface. Retain the vinegar mixture for building the final product.

4. Mix remaining 1/4 cup of vinegar, sugar, salt, and sesame oil with the remaining chopped cucumbers and carrots while the rice is cooking.

5. It's easiest to roll up the nori by placing it shiny side down on a bamboo rolling mat. Pour vinegar liquid into a reservable bowl and moisten hands. Spread 3/4 cup of rice evenly over nori, leaving a 1/2-inch border all around. It is best to spread 2 tbsp of mayonnaise equally on the rice. Mix up the vegetables and avocado, then spread the mixture evenly over the rice. Sesame seeds can be sprinkled on top. Fold the bottom third of the roll toward the center, pressing evenly throughout the roll to compress the filling. Repeat the process with a second gentle push. Toss out the rug. Using the vinegar mixture, moisten a sharp knife and cut into six equal pieces. Continue with the remaining nori sheets. Serve with the remaining pickled ginger and soy sauce that you've saved.

ZUCCHINI SUSHI

TOTAL TIME:0 HOURS 20 MINS

Ingredients

- 2 medium zucchinis
- 4 oz. cream cheese, softened.
- 1 tsp. Sriracha hot sauce
- 1 tsp. lime juice
- 1 c. lump crab meat
- 1/2 carrot, cut into thin matchsticks.
- 1/2 avocado, diced.
- 1/2 cucumber, cut into thin matchsticks.
- 1 tsp. Toasted sesame seeds

Instructions

1. Slice each zucchini into thin, flat strips using a vegetable peeler. While preparing the rest of the ingredients, place the zucchini on a platter lined with paper towels.

2. Mix the cream cheese, Sriracha, and lime juice in a medium bowl.

3. Two zucchini slices, laid up horizontally, on a cutting board (so that the long side is facing you). Layer cream cheese on top, followed by a pinch of crab, carrot, avocado, and cucumber on the left side.

4. Zucchini may be rolled up from the left side, starting at the bottom. Repeat this process with the remaining zucchini pieces and fillings. Before serving, top with sesame seeds.

AVOCADO AND MANGO QUINOA NIGIRI

PREP TIME 30 mins TOTAL TIME 30 minsPrep:1 hr Total:1 hr

| Ingredients | Instructions |

Ingredients

Quinoa Nigiri
- 1 ½ cups of organic quinoa (cooked)
- 1 tbsp organic tamari (reduced sodium, or coconut amines)
- ½ tbsp organic rice vinegar
- ½ tbsp maple syrup
- ¼ cup of raw sunflower seeds (ground into a meal)
- 1 tbsp flax meal
- 1 nori sheet (cut into 3 ½" x ¾" pieces, for wrapping around the nigiri)

Toppings
- 1 mango (fresh, cut into 2 ½" x ¾" strips)
- 1 avocado (fresh, cut into 2 ½" x ¾" strips)
- 1 jalapeño (optional, diced)
- Sriracha (optional, as need)
- 2 dashes smoked paprika (optional, +1 dash as desired)

Instructions

1. Gather your ingredients into one basin and mix thoroughly. Make sure everything is well-combined.
2. Add the flax meal and ground sunflower seeds and thoroughly combine. Make an oval out of the quinoa mixture with your hands now. In this case, wait a few minutes before serving, allowing the ingredients to come together. Troubleshooting advice is available in Chef's notes.
3. The quinoa should be formed into oval-shaped logs about 2 3/8" long and 3/8" broad using clean hands. Make a cutting board or serving plate out of each one. You'll need 12–15 quinoa sushi logs for this recipe.
4. Wrap a strip of nori sheet around the width of each one and place it in the center.
5. Top each quinoa log with a slice of mango and an avocado slice.
6. Serve with a drizzle of Sriracha and, if desired, a slice of jalapeno.
7. If you like, top with a little smoked paprika, if you have some on hand.

AVOCADO & SALMON SUSHI ROLL

Ingredients

- 2 cups of Sun Rice Japanese Style Sushi Rice
- 6 Seaweed sheets
- 1 1/2 tbsp Whole egg mayonnaise
- 1/2 tsp Wasabi
- 300g Sashimi grade salmon, cut into 6 thick strips.
- 1 Avocado, skin and stone removed, halved, and sliced.
- 1/2 tsp Soy Sauce to serve.

Instructions

1. Follow the package directions to prepare Sun Rice Sushi Rice.
2. Sushi mats should have the slats going horizontally across the surface of the mats. On the mat, lay a sheet of seaweed (shiny side down).
3. Spread 34 cups of rice over the seaweed sheet with damp hands, leaving a 3 cm wide border on the top.
4. In a bowl, combine the mayonnaise and wasabi and stir thoroughly. Place a dollop of wasabi mayo in the center of the rice and serve. Sliced avocado and a salmon strip complete the dish. Pick the mat nearest to you. As you wrap the mat over to surround the rice and filling, keep the filling firmly in place with a spoon.
5. Create five additional rolls by using the remaining seaweed sheets rice, and filling.
6. Slice sushi into 2cm-thick pieces, then serve. Serve with soy sauce and a tray of this dish on the side. Instead of salmon, you may substitute cooked peeled prawns for the fish.

BACON AND AVOCADO SUSHI ROLLS

PREP TIME 30 mins TOTAL TIME 30 minsPrep:1 hr Total:1 hr

Ingredients

- 2 cups of water
- 1 ½ tbsp of sesame oil
- 7 ounces of sushi rice
- 1 tsp rice vinegar
- 8 bacon slices
- ½ avocado, sliced for sushi
- ¼ cucumber, julienned
- 2 ounces of smoked salmon, pulled.

Instructions

1. Add 1 tbsp of sesame oil to a kettle of water, then add the sushi rice and stir. Cook for 21 minutes with the lid on.
2. Add the cooked rice, rice vinegar, and the rest of the sesame oil to a bowl and mix thoroughly. Mix until the mixture is homogeneous.
3. Lay the strips of bacon on a sushi rolling mat, gently overlapping each other.
4. Lower half of overlapping bacon strips should be evenly covered with cooked rice, so do so. The salmon, avocado, and cucumber should be placed on the lowest portion of the rice.
5. The mat may be used as a rolling surface. Cut the roll into two or three smaller pieces after trimming the excess bacon.
6. Add the rolls to a hot skillet and cook for a few minutes until they're golden brown. Cook for 2 minutes on each side.
7. Serve them as sushi on a serving plate with the sushi pieces sliced in half.

SUSHI BAKE CALIFORNIA MAKI

Prep Time: 20 mins Cook Time: 20 mins. Total Time: 40 mins

Ingredients

- SUSHI RICE
- 4 cups of freshly cooked rice
- 3 tbsp rice vinegar
- 1 tbsp sugar
- 1 tsp salt
-
- FURIKAKE
- ½ cup of sesame seeds
- ½ cup of Korean roasted seaweed crumbled or cut into small bits
- 1 tsp salt as need
- 1 tsp sugar as need
- CREAMY TOPPING
- 1 big ripe mango diced.
- 1 medium cucumber diced.
- 2 cups of Kane shredded or cut into chunks.
- 200 grams cream cheese

Instructions

RICE SUSHI

1. Small bowl: Mix Rice Vinegar with Salt and Sugar. It's time to heat it up in the microwave until the salt and sugar have dissolved completely.
2. In a bowl, combine the cooked rice with the ingredients and stir thoroughly until the rice is equally coated.

FURIKAKE

3. Toast the sesame seeds over low heat until they are aromatic and golden. Add the nori crumbles and combine well. Infuse with salt and sugar.

CHRISTMAS CREMESIZE

4. Mix the cream cheese, Japanese mayonnaise, and Sriracha together in a dish before serving.
5. Add the chopped Kane, 34 of the mangos, and 34 of the cucumber to the mixture. Remember to save some mango and cucumber for subsequent use. The amount of salt you use is up to you.

THE ASSEMBLY OF BAKED SUSHI

6. Spread the sushi rice out evenly in an 8x6-inch pan, then softly press it down. Cover rice with a thin coating of Bukkake, making sure it is well covered.

- ¼ cup of Japanese mayonnaise
- 1 tbsp Sriracha - adjust as desired.
- salt as need
- 20 sheets Korean roasted seaweed sheets - or use nori sheets.

7. Spread the creamy topping over the entire surface. Top with the leftover mango and cucumber pieces, as well as a few sprinkles of Fricke. If desired, drizzle with Japan Mayonnaise and Sriracha.

8. Bake for 20 minutes at 200°C. Simply spoon some out and wrap in nori to enjoy.

SUSHI BAKE CALIFORNIA MAKI

Cook Time 48 minutes. Total Time 48 minutes

Ingredients

- 2 cups of spelt, white, or oat flour.
- 1 tsp baking soda
- 3/4 tsp each: cinnamon, baking powder, and salt.
- 1 1/2 cup of mashed banana (360g)
- 1 cup of diced apple (120g)
- 1/2 cup of pure maple syrup, honey, or agave
- 1/4 cup of milk of choice
- 1/4 cup of oil
- tsp pure vanilla extract

Instructions

1. The oven should be preheated at 350 degrees Fahrenheit. Prepare a 9-by-5-inch baking dish with cooking spray. To make a batter, combine the dry components first, then the wet. Pour into the frying pan and smooth down the surface. 48 minutes on the center rack, or until puffed and tender. Keep cool. The flavor and texture are much better the second day, so if you have the patience, refrigerate overnight.

BBQ SUSHI ROLL BY PIT BUDDIES BBQ

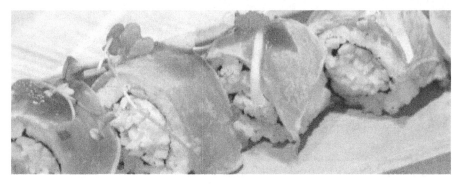

Ingredients

- 1/3 lb., breakfast sausage
- 1 block, cheese (cut in 1/4" square strips)
- 1 jalapeno thinly sliced.
- 1 red onion thinly sliced.
- 1 bottle, Hasty-Bake BBQ sauce
- 6-9 pieces, bacon
- Bamboo sushi roller

Instructions

1. Bacon should be sliced to roughly 9/10 of the sushi roller length.
2. The sushi roller may be used to roll the bacon. Try to keep the bacon layer as even as possible.
3. Uncooked breakfast sausage can be spread over the bacon, leaving approximately half an inch of the bacon visible. The bottom of the roll should be the furthest away from you, and the exposed end should be at the bottom.
4. About a quarter inch in from the left and right edges, arrange the cheese, jalapeño, and red onion slices. Keep these components as close together as you can. One strip across the roll is all you need. The jalapeño, red onion, and cheese will all be leftover.
5. Begin to coil the bamboo around the cheese and veggies, starting at one end. Keep your cylinder as tight as you can.
6. Make a tight roll by tucking the bamboo beneath itself.
7. Using your hands, lift the bamboo and continue to roll it up.

8. Charcoal may be lit in the Hasty-Bake Charcoal Grill in a matter of minutes. Put a few chunks of smoking wood (apple, hickory, oak, pecan, and cherry pair nicely with pork) on the embers after the temperature is stable around 325°-350°.

9. To cook the BBQ sushi roll, just place it on the grill grates. The bacon will crisp faster if you rotate the sushi roll every 5 to 7 minutes. During the last 5-10 minutes of cooking, drizzle on some BBQ sauce.

10. Remove the sushi roll from the Hasty-Bake Charcoal Grill and let it sit for 5-10 minutes once the sauce has set. Now it's time to eat!

11. The "filling" may be made with any of your favorite cheeses, veggies, or other components.

REDNECK SUSHI

Prep time: 15 minutes Cook time: 20 minutes.

Ingredients

- Bacon
- Hamburger-Venison
- alapeno's
- String cheese/any type

Instructions

1. When you're ready to make your hamburger or venison or whatever you'd want, spread your bacon out on a mat and get to mixing!
2. Then season your meat with some hot sauce.
3. The meat should be flattened into the bacon before being wrapped.
4. Add some jalapenos and a hard cheese to the middle of the meat.
5. Roll it up, then cook it at a steady heat for a while (hot coals on the grill)
6. Add some barbecue sauce when it's almost done cooking.
7. Slice it up and eat it with fried onions and peppers when it's done. To eat it with, don't forget the toothpicks.

AJI NANBANZUKE SPICY HORSE MACKEREL WITH VEGETABLES

Prep time: 15 minutes Cook time: 20 minutes.

Ingredients

- 3 horse mackerel fillets
- 1 onion
- 1 carrot
- 2 bell peppers
- 3 tbsp potato starch or corn flour
- pinch of salt and pepper
- oil for frying
- for the marinade:
- 50ml sushi vinegar
- 1 tbsp mirin rice wine
- 1 tbsp's sake
- 1 1/2 tbsp soy sauce
- 1 red chili pepper, dried

Instructions

1. Make thin circles out of the red chili pepper. Mix all of the marinade ingredients together and store in an airtight container.

2. Cut all the veggies into strips that are about the same width.

3. Heat a little oil in a frying pan on medium high. Sauté the veggies for 5 minutes, depending on their tenderness. The marinade should be added to the pan and lightly tossed after the pan has been removed from the heat. Remove from consideration.

4. Use some kitchen paper to pat the fish fillets dry. Salt and pepper the fillets on both sides. After that, dust with potato starch or corn flour to finish dusting.

5. Heat some frying oil to 180°C in a pot. Carefully drop a few fillets into the oil one at a time, skin side down, and cook for about two minutes. Adding too many fillets to a hot pan will result in mushy, greasy fish. Avoid overcrowding the pan. Remove the fillets from the pan and cook the remaining fillets until they are done.

6. Place the fillets on a platter and top with the marinated veggies when ready to serve. For a complete supper, combine with rice.

INARI SUSHI

Prep time: 15 minutes Cook time: 20 minutes.

Ingredients

- inari deep-fried tofu pockets.
- Japanese sushi rice
- sesame seeds
- shiitake mushrooms
- carrots

Instructions

1. The rice for sushi should be made in advance.
2. Open an inari tofu pocket and place a ball of sushi rice inside once it has been made and chilled.
3. Adding sesame seeds and soy sauce and wasabi to inari sushi makes it a tasty addition to a variety of other sushi rolls. You can also pack them in bento boxes with some veggies for an easy lunch.
4. Cook the carrots and soak the dried shiitake mushrooms before slicing them up into small pieces if you want to spice up your inari. Fill your tofu pouches with this mixture of rice and these two ingredients.

TERIYAKI CHICKEN SUSHI ROLLS

prep time: 45 M cook time: 25 M. total time: 1 HOUR 10 M

Ingredients

FOR RICE:
- 2 cups of sushi rice
- 4 cups of water
- Rice vinegar

FOR TERIYAKI CHICKEN:
- 1 boneless, skinless chicken breast
- Bottled teriyaki sauce.
- Sesame oil
- Brown sugar

FOR SUSHI ROLLS:
- 5 sheets of seaweed
- Chicken
- 1 avocado
- 5 fresh asparagus spears

ON THE SIDE:
- Pickled ginger
- Wasabi
- Sriracha mayonnaise
- Sriracha mayonnaise
- Fried onions (I got mine at an Indian grocery store)

Instructions

1. Sushi rice should be made ahead of time. Rinse the rice in cold water before cooking it. A heavy-duty saucepan filled with water is required. Bring to a boil on medium-high heat. Cover and bring to a simmer. Cook the rice for 15 to 20 minutes, or until it is tender but still firm to the bite. Allow to cool before serving. Once the rice has cooled, drizzle it with 1 to 2 tbsp of rice vinegar. Set aside until you're ready to put the rolls together.

2. To cook teriyaki chicken, follow these instructions. Chicken breasts can be diced into thin slices. In a plastic bag, combine the chicken, sesame oil, and a touch of brown sugar with a few drops of teriyaki sauce. Place all ingredients in a zip-top bag and refrigerate for about an hour to marinate. For 3 to 4 minutes, sauté the chicken in a small amount of olive oil until it's cooked through and slightly crispy on the surface, but still moist within. Set aside to cool when you've removed it from the pan.

3. How to make sushi rolls: Lay the seaweed shiny side down on a sushi mat. Add a layer of sushi rice on top (enough so that the seaweed is covered, leaving the top inch or so bare) Add the remaining ingredients to your taste (chicken, avocado slices, and asparagus). Check out the photo in this post for an example. You don't want the sushi to break apart when you slice it, so begin rolling the sushi from top to bottom, being sure to maintain the roll tight. Continue with the rest of the rolls. Each of these ingredients should yield about five cinnamon buns.

4. When ready to cut, cover the rolls in plastic wrap and put them in the fridge. Cut each roll into eight thin pieces using a sharp knife. Include ginger and wasabi in your dish as an added finishing touch.

URAMAKI INSIDE OUT SUSHI ROLL

prep time: 45 M cook time: 25 M. total time: 1 HOUR 10 M

Ingredients

- 660g cooked Japanese sushi rice.
- 50ml sushi vinegar
- for the inside out roll:
- 1 long strip of sashimi-grade fish
- 1 long strip of cucumber
- 1 sheet nori seaweed
- 1 sprig dill
- 1/2 tsp wasabi
- to serve:
- 1 tbsp soy sauce

Instructions

1. To keep the rice from sticking, wet the interior of a big bowl or a sushi rice mixing bowl. When making sushi, you must use freshly cooked, piping-hot rice.

2. In a bowl, combine the rice with the sushi vinegar. Using a rice paddle, gently integrate the vinegar into the rice until it is thoroughly absorbed. Wait until room temperature for the sushi rice to cool. To keep the sushi rice from drying out, wrap it in a tea towel dampened with water.

3. Place one half of the nori seaweed on the sushi mat shiny side down after cutting it in half. For the most part, it's best to put sushi's glossy side out on the plate.

4. Spread 110 grams of sushi rice equally over the nori seaweed. Add a sprig of dill to the rice and serve. Assuming that the nori seaweed is facing up, turn the sushi rice over. Place the two cucumber strips and the sashimi-grade fish in the middle of the wasabi-topped plate.

5. Beginning from one end, wrap the dough up and tuck in the roll's edge to completely cover the filling. Roll the sushi in a tight cylinder by lifting the mat's edge and pushing it forward.

6. Slice the roll into six equal pieces using a sharp knife that has been gently moistened. The first step is to cut it in half and then into thirds. To prevent the rice from sticking to the knife, wipe it off with a moist cloth between each cut.

7. Soy sauce is a must. Garnish with white or black sesame seeds, tobiko, chives, or whatever else you choose.

KETO BACON SUSHI

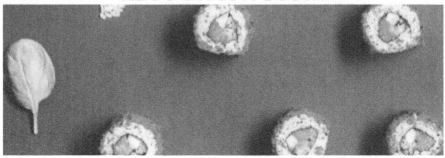

Ingredients

- 6 slices bacon, halved.
- 2 Persian cucumbers thinly sliced.
- 2 medium carrots thinly sliced.
- 1 avocado, sliced.
- 4 oz. cream cheese, softened.
- Sesame seeds, for garnish

Instructions

1. Preheat the oven to 400 degrees Fahrenheit. Set up a cooling rack on a baking sheet lined with aluminum foil. Place the bacon halves in an equal layer on a baking sheet and bake for 11 to 13 minutes, or until crisp but still malleable.

2. Cut the cucumbers, carrots, and avocado into chunks around the width of the bacon in the meanwhile.

3. Set aside to cool completely, then evenly spread cream cheese over each piece of bacon. Place the veggies on one end of the bacon and distribute evenly. Vegetables should be firmly rolled.

4. Immediately before serving, sprinkle the dish with sesame seeds.

ASIAN LETTUCE WRAPS

Prep:20 mins Cook:15 mins Total:35 mins

Ingredients

- 16 Boston Bibb or butter lettuce leaves
- 1-pound lean ground beef
- 1 tbsp cooking oil
- 1 large onion, chopped.
- ¼ cup of hoisin sauce
- 2 cloves fresh garlic, minced.
- 1 tbsp soy sauce
- 1 tbsp rice wine vinegar
- 2 tsp minced pickled ginger.
- 1 dash Asian Chile pepper sauce, or as need (Optional)
- 1 can water chestnuts, drained, and finely chopped.
- 1 bunch green onions, chopped.
- 2 tsp Asian (dark) sesame oil

Instructions

1. Make sure not to rip the lettuce leaves as you rinse and dry them. Take from consideration.
2. Medium-high heat in a big skillet. In a high pan, brown the beef and stir in the cooking oil until crumbled, 5 to 7 minutes. Transfer the meat to a bowl, and then drain and discard the fat. While meat is cooking, cook onion in same skillet for 5 to 10 minutes, stirring often. In a bowl, combine onions with hoisin sauce and all the other sauces. Using a wok or large skillet over medium-high heat, sauté the water chestnuts and green onions for 2 minutes, stirring often.
3. Stack a big serving dish with lettuce leaves on its outside edge and a heaping portion of meat in the middle.

SEAFOOD CHIRASHI SUSHI

Prep Time: 30 minutes Cook Time: 30 minutes. Total Time: 1 hour

Ingredients

- 310 grams Japanese short-grain rice 1 1/2 cups of
- 1 1/2 cups of cold water
- 1/4 cup mikan Natural Rice Vinegar
- 3 tbsp sugar
- 1 tsp salt
- 85 grams snap peas (14 pods, trimmed)
- 100 grams carrot (1/2 carrot peeled & sliced into 12 coins)
- 180 grams shrimp (31-40, peeled and deveined)
- 3 large eggs
- 1 pinch salt
- 1 tsp vegetable oil
- 160 grams sashimi-grade fish (such as tuna, salmon, or Hamachi)
- 2 tsp toasted sesame seeds
- 100 grams Kura

Instructions

1. Cold, running water should be used to wash the rice in a sieve until the water runs mainly clear. Next, drain the rice and combine it with 1 1/2 cups of water in a large, lidded pot. While you prepare the toppings, let this sit for 30 minutes.

2. Addition of water to sushi rice in a saucepan.

3. Add rice vinegar, sugar and salt to a blender or food processor, blend until smooth.

4. Making sushi vinegar in a glass jar using chopsticks.

5. Cook the carrots in salted water until tender, then drain and set aside. Fork-tender carrots are ready when they can be poked with a fork. Cook the snap peas for around 30 seconds once they've been added. Transfer them to an ice water bath using a slotted spoon, then wait until they are totally cooled before removing them.

6. Snap peas with boiled carrots.

7. Remove the shrimp from the boiling water and set aside. Poach the shrimp until they are bright orange and no longer transparent in the boiling water (about 2-3 minutes). Drain and then chill in a water bath.

8. Shrimp that has been boiled.

9. Beat the eggs with chopsticks until they are all the same hue, taking care not to generate air bubbles.
10. Whipping an egg yolk in a bowl with chopsticks.
11. Cook the beef on a nonstick skillet until browned but not burnt. Spread the oil out evenly and wipe away any excess with a paper towel before serving.
12. Stir the egg until it coated the pan's bottom. Be patient and allow the edges to dry out before moving it to another pan. After that, use a spatula to turn the egg over. After a few seconds, cover the egg with plastic wrap and chop it up on a cutting board. Stack the remaining eggs on top of each other and repeat the process with them.
13. Making a thin omelet using eggs for Chirashi Sushi's omelets topping.
14. After the eggs are cooked, stack them and cut them into thin threads using a sharp knife.
15. Toppers for chirashi sushi, such as egg or kinship tam ago threads.
16. Until you're ready to serve it, cut the fish into bite-sized cubes and store it in the refrigerator. Carrots and snap peas can also be sliced into flowers or leaves if desired.
17. Sushi garnished with snap peas sliced into leaves.
18. After soaking the rice, bring it to a boil over high heat and let it simmer for a few minutes. Set a timer for 15 minutes and reduce the heat to low as soon as it reaches a boil.
19. Cover the pan and set a timer for 10 minutes. Remove the pan from the oven.
20. Rice should be transferred to a pot and the sushi vinegar should be drenched equally throughout. Fold the sushi vinegar into the rice with a spatula or rice paddle, taking careful note to squish up the rice grains.
21. Refrigerate while folding to fast bring the rice to room temperature once the vinegar is entirely incorporated.
22. Mixing sushi rice in a bowl.
23. Set up 4 serving bowls of Chirashi Sushi and top each with a sprinkling of sesame seeds.
24. Topped with toasted sesame seeds, sushi rice bowls.
25. Sprinkle the rice with the shredded egg and then add the fish, shrimp, and veggies on top of it.
26. Ikura and soy sauce are available for sprinkling if desired.

CALIFORNIA ROLL

Prep Time:35 mins Cook Time:0 mins

Ingredients	Instructions

Ingredients

- 1 cup of sushi rice, short grain, rinsed and drained.
- 1 cup of water
- 1 tbsp. rice vinegar
- 1 tbsp. sugar
- 1 tbsp. salt
- 2-4 sheets nori, seaweed
- 2 tbsp. toasted sesame seeds.
- 1 small carrot, peeled and sliced into matchstick-sized pieces.
- 1 small cucumber, peeled and sliced into matchstick-sized pieces.
- 1 avocado, peeled, pitted, and thinly sliced.
- 2 imitation crab sticks
- wasabi, soy sauce, sriracha

Instructions

1. Add 1 cup of water to a saucepan and cook the rice. Bring the mixture to a rolling boil.
2. When water reaches a boil, cover the pan, and turn the heat down. Add an extra 15 minutes to your cooking time.
3. Let the pan sit covered for five minutes before turning off the flame.
4. 30-60 seconds in the microwave should be enough to dissolve the vinegar, sugar, and salt. Stir the ingredients into the rice until it is thoroughly coated. Set the rice aside to cool fully.
5. Use plastic wrap to cover your sushi mat. Using plastic wrap, lay a nori sheet shiny side up on a work surface. Have water and your other items ready to go, as well as a place to store them.
6. Dip your fingers in water and spread 14-inch-thick sticky rice on a flat surface with a uniform layer. The nori sheet should be pressed into the spread nearly all the way to the edge.
7. Toss the rice with around 12 tbsp. toasted sesame seeds.
8. The rice side should be on the bottom of the nori sheet when you carefully flip it over.

- bamboo sushi mat, I found a bamboo placemat at the Dollar Store, and it worked great!
- plastic wrap
- a bowl of water
- chopsticks

9. Spread about 1/3 of the nori sheet with a layer of filling, going all the way across.
10. Fold the sushi mat over the nori by 12 inches and place it on the sushi mat.
11. Unroll the nori and draw it to the mat's edge once again.
12. Continue rolling and unrolling the mat until all of the filling has been rolled over.
13. Using your hands, tightly wrap the mat around the roll, pushing down forcefully to ensure a tight seal.
14. Refrigerate the roll for about 30 minutes after wrapping it in a plastic bag.
15. Slice with a very sharp knife after removing from the fridge. Make slices approximately one inch thick by slicing off both ends.
16. With a little sriracha if you prefer it hot, soy sauce and wasabi should accompany your California Rolls.

HALLOWEEN SALMON TEMARI SUSHI

Ingredients

- 250g cooked Japanese rice.
- 1 tbsp sushi vinegar
- smoked salmon.
- nori seaweed sheets
- wasabi paste.
- soy sauce and pickled sushi ginger, to serve.

Instructions

1. If you want to make sushi, you'll need to start by cooking your rice, anyway you choose. After the rice has cooled somewhat, toss in the sushi vinegar.

2. Slices of salmon should be placed in the center of the cling film after the rice has been cooked. Then, place a tbsp of rice on the salmon and twist the film to form a ball of rice.

3. Finally, garnish your salmon with nori seaweed cut into Halloween-themed forms, such as pumpkins, witch hats, or anything else you can think of.

CALIFORNIA ROLL

Prep: 45 min Inactive: 1 hr Cook: 20 min

Ingredients

- Juice of 1/2 lemon
- 1 medium avocado, peeled, pitted.
- 4 sheets nori
- 1/2 batch sushi rice, recipe follows.
- 1/3 cup of sesame seeds, toasted.
- 1 small cucumber, peeled, seeded.
- 4 crabsticks, torn into pieces.
- Pickled ginger, for serving.
- Wasabi, for serving.
- Soy sauce, for serving.

Sushi Rice:

- 2 cups of sushi
- 2 cups of water, +extra for rinsing rice
- 2 tbsp rice vinegar
- 2 tbsp sugar
- 1 tbsp kosher salt

Instructions

1. To keep the avocado from turning brown, drizzle the avocado with lemon juice.
2. Use plastic wrap to cover a bamboo rolling mat. Crosswise, divide nori sheets into two halves. On the plastic mat, place a nori sheet with the glossy side down. Spread roughly half a cup of rice on the nori with your fingers wet with water. Sprinkle sesame seeds on the rice. Look at the rice side of the nori sheet and flip it over. A quarter of a sheet should be filled with the cucumber, avocado, and crab sticks. Keeping the contents in place with your fingers, begin by grabbing the mat's nearest edge and rolling it into a tight cylinder. Let go of the mat and put it away. A moist towel can be used to protect the surface. Rep till all rice is gone. Cut each roll into six equal pieces. ' Pickled ginger, wasabi, and soy sauce are all great accompaniments.

It's called sushi rice:

3. In a mixing basin, add the rice and cold water and stir thoroughly. Drain and repeat 2 to 3 times, or until the water clears, depending on the rice.

4. The rice and 2 cups of water should be placed in a medium-sized pot and brought to a boil over high heat. Fill the saucepan halfway with water, cover, and bring to a boil over high heat. Turn the heat down to the lowest level and cover the pot after the water has reached a rolling boil. About 15 minutes later, add in the veggies. Once you've removed the dish from the heat let it sit for 10 minutes with the lid on.

5. A bowl with rice vinegar, sugar, and salt is needed. A microwave for 30–45 seconds Mix the rice and vinegar in a big basin. Fold the rice completely to coat each grain in the mixture. Before making sushi or sashimi, let the fish cool down to room temperature.

CALIFORNIA ROLLS WITH SALMON AND CREAM CHEESE

Ingredients

- 540 ml Rice
- 7 tbsp ⬜ Sushi vinegar
- 3 1/2 tbsp ⬜ Sugar
- 1 tsp ⬜ Salt
- 1 Toasted white sesame seeds
- 1 Mayonnaise
- 1 Avocado
- 1 Cucumber
- 8 stick Imitation crab sticks
- 1 Smoked salmon
- 1 Cream cheese
- 2 sheets Toasted nori seaweed.

Instructions

1. Freshly cooked rice and the ingredients are combined to produce sushi rice. Four halves of a nori seaweed sheet

2. Slice the avocado and cucumber into eighths, then prepare the remaining ingredients for the fillings.

3. Step 2 of the recipe for California Rolls with Cream Cheese and Salmon.

4. Align the bottom ends of a sushi mat with a piece of plastic wrap. Rice should be placed on top of the sesame seeds, which should be spread out around 15cm wide on the bottom end.

5. A nori seaweed piece sliced into fours should be placed just above the rice's center. Line the nori seaweed with mayonnaise.

6. a step-by-step pictorial of the California Rolls with Cream Cheese and Salmon recipe.

7. Leave a little strip of rice at the bottom of the avocado, cucumber, and crab sticks.

8. To begin rolling, press down on the cucumber sticks in the middle, and then raise the bottom end of the sushi mat.

9. Maintaining a clean edge is essential when using plastic wrap. The sushi roll should be squeezed through the sushi rolling mat.

10. Use your fingers to tuck the rice in at the end of the roll while pressing down on the sushi rolling mat.

11. Step 8 photo of the recipe for the salmon and cream cheese California rolls

12. Discard the sushi rolling mat. Make three more rolls by using the same procedure. Allowing the rolls to rest for a few minutes before slicing will result in cleaner slices.

13. California Rolls with Cream Cheese and Salmon Recipe Step 9

14. Make four smoked salmon and cream cheese wraps in the same way.

15. To make cleanup a breeze, cut the end of the plastic wrap away from the roll. Slice the roll into eight pieces while the plastic wrap is still on. Remove the plastic film.

16. To make salmon and cream cheese stuffed California rolls, follow these steps:

17. To make rainbow rolls, simply add additional toppings to the standard California rolls.!

MAKE SUSHI CAKE AND WIN THE HOLIDAYS

Ingredients

- Rice
- 3 cups of short grain (sushi) rice
- 3 cups of water
- Sushi Vinegar
- 2 tbsp rice vinegar (not seasoned)
- 1 tbsp sugar
- ¾ tsp kosher salt
- Pink Rice Seasoning
- ¼ cup of museum (plum vinegar)
- 1 tsp shiso powder

Instructions

1. Rinse the rice in many changes of cool water until the water runs clear in a heavy-bottomed saucepan. Remove all of the rinse water from the sink. Add the 3 quarts of water to the mixture.

2. Place a tight-fitting lid on the saucepan. This cover should not be removed until the rice has been cooked.

3. A thorough boil is required. If the lid is on tight, you'll hear it rumble, see steam escaping from the edges, and the water may even boil over. Set a timer for 18 minutes and the lowest heat setting on the stove.

4. Make the seasoned vinegar while the rice is cooking. Shake the vinegar, sugar, and salt together in a container until they are completely dissolved, and then set aside.

5. For one minute after the timer goes off, put the heat all the way back up to high and wait for any residual water to start boiling again. Five minutes after the heat has been turned off, leave the cover on the pot (if your stove is electric, remove the pot from the burner).

6. After 5 minutes, remove the lid and use chopsticks or a rice paddle to fluff the rice. Half the rice should be placed on a big chopping board or in a large dish.
7. If possible, enlist the assistance of a buddy. orr family member to help you sprinkle the seasoned vinegar on the rice and toss it to coat it uniformly while also using a fan to chill it (a small rectangle of cardboard makes an effective fan). Mix the vinegar using a rice paddle in a cutting motion so that you don't shatter the rice. When the rice is evenly seasoned, shiny, and dry, it is ready to use.
8. Use sushi vinegar and shiso powder to season the remaining half of the rice in.

MAKE SUSHI CAKE AND WIN THE HOLIDAYS

Ingredients

- Rice
- 3 cups of short grain (sushi) rice
- 3 cups of water
- Sushi Vinegar
- 2 tbsp rice vinegar (not seasoned)
- 1 tbsp sugar
- ¾ tsp kosher salt
- Pink Rice Seasoning
- ¼ cup of museum (plum vinegar)
- 1 tsp shiso powder

Instructions

1. Rinse the rice in many changes of cool water until the water runs clear in a heavy-bottomed saucepan. Remove all of the rinse water from the sink. Add the 3 quarts of water to the mixture.

2. Place a tight-fitting lid on the saucepan. This cover should not be removed until the rice has been cooked.

3. A thorough boil is required. If the lid is on tight, you'll hear it rumble, see steam escaping from the edges, and the water may even boil over. Set a timer for 18 minutes and the lowest heat setting on the stove.

4. Make the seasoned vinegar while the rice is cooking. Shake the vinegar, sugar, and salt together in a container until they are completely dissolved, and then set aside.

5. For one minute after the timer goes off, put the heat all the way back up to high and wait for any residual water to start boiling again. Five minutes after the heat has been turned off, leave the cover on the pot (if your stove is electric, remove the pot from the burner).

CALIFORNIA SUSHI BOWLS

Prep T: 8 minutes Cook Time: 15 minutes Total Time: 23 minutes

Ingredients

- 1 1/2 cups of Calrose Sushi Rice
- 2 cups of water
- 1/4 cup of seasoned rice vinegar Malukan
- 1/4 cup of Japanese mayonnaise
- 2 tsp sriracha
- 8 oz imitation crab
- 1/2 cup of diced English cucumber.
- 1-2 nori sheets chopped.
- 1 large avocado peeled and sliced.
- Black and toasted sesame seeds
- 1/4 cup of low-sodium soy sauce for serving
- Nori Fricke

Instructions

1. Prepare the sushi rice by sifting 1 1/2 cups of it through a mesh sieve. After thoroughly rinsing the rice, place it in the rice cooker with 2 cups of water. Afterwards, set the rice cooker to "on."

2. Using a baking sheet with a rim, transfer the cooked rice.

3. Next, add 1/4 cup of seasoned rice vinegar to the rice and mix it in until evenly distributed. To execute this, you'll need a rice paddle. Make sure you don't mush up the rice by squeezing it too hard. Then allow the rice to cool fully.

4. Create a spicy mayo by blending 1/4 cup Japanese mayonnaise with 2 teaspoon Sriracha.

5. Cucumber and imitation crab meat, both 8-ounce cups, are chopped now. Additionally, a few Nori pieces can be smashed (dried seaweed).

6. Add the crab, cucumber, and avocado slices to a bowl once the sushi rice has cooled. Then add the spicy mayonnaise and finish with the nori, sesame seeds, and furikake, which are all diced up.

CALIFORNIA HAND ROLL

Cook Time 20 mins. Total Time 20 mins

Ingredients

- 8 toasted nori sheets
- 1-pound cooked lump crab meat
- 2 scallions thinly sliced.
- 2 tbsp paleo mayonnaise
- ½ tsp red pepper flakes optional
- 1 tbsp lime juice
- Diamond Crystal kosher salt
- Freshly ground black pepper
- 1 large Hass avocado pitted, peeled, and thinly sliced.
- 2 small Japanese or Persian cucumbers cut into matchsticks.
- Handful of radish sprouts or microgreens
- 2 tbsp toasted sesame seeds

Instructions

1. Toasting the nori sheets can be skipped if you're short on time, although even toasted nori might benefit from a little heat.
2. Slowly fan each nori sheet back and forth over a gas flame until the color turns vivid green.
3. Is there no gas stove? Toasting nori in the oven is another option. Turn on the broiler with the rack approximately 6 inches from the heating element and broil for a few seconds. Just 10 seconds in the oven is all it takes to roast two pieces of nori on a baking sheet and render them a bright green.
4. Toast the nori by halving each piece of nori in half horizontally.
5. Crabmeat, scallions, mayonnaise, red pepper flakes (if used), and lime juice should be mixed in a big bowl. Toss in the seasonings to taste, then mix completely.
6. Put the nori shiny side down and ladle 2 tbsp of crab mixture onto the left side of the rectangle to make each roll. Roll up and serve. From the top left corner to bottom right corner of the nori, the filling should flow diagonally over the nori.

7. Add avocado, cucumber, and sprouts to the crab before serving. To construct a cone, begin by folding the bottom left corner of the nori over the crab and vegetable mixture.

8. Sprinkle with toasted sesame seeds and eat right away—don't allow the nori to become soggy!

SUSHI RICE AND CALIFORNIA ROLLS RECIPE

Prep : 1 hour Cook T: 20 minutes. Total T: 1 hour 20 minutes

Ingredients

- 2 cups of Japanese short or medium grain rice
- 2 1/2 cups of cold water
- 5 Tbsp Sushi Vinegar
- 4 Tbsp Rice vinegar
- 2 Tbsp sugar
- 2 tsp salt, I used sea salt.
- 1/2 lb. Imitation crab meat
- 1 Avocado, ripe but still firm
- 1/2 medium cucumber, peeled.
- Toasted Nori Seaweed
- Toasted sesame seeds
- Soy sauce, regular
- Wasabi paste.
- For spicy mayo: Mayonnaise, ~1 Tbsp and Sriracha hot chili sauce (~1 tsp) or as need.

Instructions

1. Using a Rice Maker or Stovetop, here's how to make the perfect sushi rice: P.S. Don't add salt to your rice while it's cooking.

2. Rinse the rice well under cold water to remove any remaining scum. Drain the water well. Follow the manufacturer's directions for your rice cooker and select the white rice option before moving on to step.

3. Add 2 cups of cold water to 2 cups of drained rice in a large, heavy saucepan. Increase the heat and cover the pan to bring the contents to a rolling boil. Over medium-low heat, cover and cook until all the water is gone (7-8 min). Rather of removing the lid to check for bubbles, keep an ear out for a sudden cessation of bubbling.

4. Immediately after hearing a tiny hissing sound, lower the heat and cook for a further 6 minutes. Wait 15 minutes before serving. For the most part, this is the white rice that is served with most Japanese dishes.

5. Break up the clumps of hot rice by transferring it to a big bowl and smashing it with your hands.

6. Stir in the chilled sushi vinegar once the rice has been allowed to come to room temperature.
7. You're going to need these ingredients to make your California Rolls.
8. To keep your sushi matt clean and reusable, you should first cover it in plastic wrap.
9. Split the nori into two pieces by folding it in half.
10. Cook the sesame seeds until golden brown, stirring often, in a medium saucepan. Slice the vegetables.
11. A substantial amount of sushi rice should be spread on the nori sheet. The rice should be distributed uniformly throughout the nori using damp fingertips (to keep your fingertips wet to avoid sticking).
12. Make sure that the rice side of the nori sheet is facing down by flipping it over (this way, your rice will be on the outside). Take a sheet of rice and spread your fillings evenly across it. Then, wrap the rice into a cylinder.
13. Use your matt to keep the roll in place as you begin rolling away from you. Make a tight roll by putting some pressure on it. It will be tough to cut if it is not sufficiently tight. Before turning the roll over, sprinkle the sesame seeds on top while it's still on the mat.
14. The rice will not adhere to your knife if you run it through a moist paper towel first. Slice the roll into 1-inch rings after cutting it in half. Using a sharp knife, I've found that slicing swiftly helps.

CALIFORNIA ROLL

Total Time: 10 min

Ingredients

- 2 sheets nori (dried seaweed), cut in half.
- 4 cups of prepared sushi rice
- 1 Tbsp. sesame seeds
- 1 1/2 cups of cups of fresh crab meat
- 1 small cucumber, cut into large matchsticks.
- 1 ripe, Fresh California Avocado, seeded, peeled, and cut into 16 slices.
- 2 Tbsp. tobiko/ white fish roe
- Wasabi, optional
- Pickled ginger, optional
- Tamari or soy sauce for serving, optional.

Instructions

1. Put the nori (seaweed) on a bamboo roller covered in plastic. To prevent sushi rice from sticking to your hands, wet them with cold water. One cup of sushi rice, made as directed, should be used to cover the seaweed evenly.

2. Add a quarter of the sesame seeds to the dish. The bamboo roller should be left in place while you flip the nori over so that the rice is in direct touch with the plastic wrap.

3. You can start by laying out a quarter of a cup of crab meat, cucumber, and avocado on one side of the nori. With the bamboo roller, roll the sushi away from you as much as possible.

4. Use a moist cloth to clean the knife after each cut and use a very sharp knife to cut the sushi in two. Repeat the process of halving and halving until you have 8 pieces.

5. Keep your blade clean by wiping it between each cut.

6. To finish, sprinkle some tobiko over each slice. Repeat the procedure with the remaining components.

7. A substantial amount of sushi rice should be spread on the nori sheet. The rice should be distributed uniformly throughout the nori using damp fingertips (to keep your fingertips wet to avoid sticking).
8. Make sure that the rice side of the nori sheet is facing down by flipping it over (this way, your rice will be on the outside). Take a sheet of rice and spread your fillings evenly across it. Then, wrap the rice into a cylinder.
9. Use your matt to keep the roll in place as you begin rolling away from you. Make a tight roll by putting some pressure on it. It will be tough to cut if it is not sufficiently tight. Before turning the roll over, sprinkle the sesame seeds on top while it's still on the mat.
10. The rice will not adhere to your knife if you run it through a moist paper towel first. Slice the roll into 1-inch rings after cutting it in half. Using a sharp knife, I've found that slicing swiftly helps.

TUNA SALAD SUSHI ROLL

Prep: 30 mins Cook: 0 mins Total: 30 mins

Ingredients

- 1 tbsp finely chopped onion.
- 2/3 cup of canned tuna
- 1 tbsp mayonnaise
- 1 dash salt
- 1 tsp Japanese hot mustard (karahi), optional
- 4 sheets nori (dried seaweed)
- 6 cups of cooked sushi rice
- Gari shogi (sweet, pickled ginger), for garnish
- 2 tsp toasted and/or black sesame seeds, optional.
- Soy sauce, for serving.

Instructions

1. To create the tuna salad, in a bowl, combine the chopped onion, tuna, mayonnaise, and salt. Alternatively, you can make tuna salad according to your preferred recipe. If you want a spicy tuna salad, stir in a teaspoon of karashi mustard to the tuna salad mixture.

2. Avoid seaweed and stray grains by covering the bamboo mat with plastic wrap. This also simplifies cleaning. One nori sheet should be placed on top of the bamboo mat.

3. 1/4 cup sushi rice on top of the nori sheet Spread a line of tuna salad horizontally over the rice in the center.

4. Roll up the bamboo mat, pressing forward to form a cylinder out of the sushi. Remove the bamboo mat from the sushi by pressing it hard. Rep the procedure to create additional tuna salad rolls.

5. Before slicing sushi, wipe the knife with a damp towel. Sushi rolls should be cut into bite-size pieces. Serve with soy sauce and garnish with gari shoga and sesame seeds, if using.

MINI CUCUMBER SUSHI ROLLS

Prep: 30 mins Total: 30 mins

Ingredients

- 1 long seedless cucumber ends trimmed.
- 1 carrot, shredded.
- 1 (4 ounce) package cream cheese, softened
- ¼ cup of raisins
- 24 long fresh chives for tying

Instructions

1. Slice the cucumber into 8 1/8-inch-long strips with a peeler. Each slice should be cut in half lengthwise, then in thirds.

2. On the bottom edge of a cucumber slice, spread 1 tbsp. of cream cheese and push 2 or 3 raisins into the cream cheese with your fingers. Start at the filled end of the cucumber slice and roll it up like a sushi roll. Tie a chive around the roll to keep it in place. Replicate with the rest of the components.

RAW CARROT SUSHI

Prep: 30 mins Total: 30 mins

Ingredients

- 2 Nori seaweed sheets
- 4 carrots
- 1/2 avocado
- 1/2 bell pepper (red, yellow, etc.)
- 1/3 kohlrabi

Instructions

1. Cut the veggies into sticks, starting with the avocado, then moving on to the bell pepper and kohlrabi (or julienne).

2. Put the carrots in a food processor after peeling and slicing them. Carrots should be processed until they are uniform in texture and resemble rice.

3. Instead of sushi rice, spread the shredded carrot on the Nori sheet. Press firmly until it adheres to the seaweed, then check to see whether it's been spread out properly.

4. On top of the carrot layer, add the remaining veggies.

5. Like a traditional sushi roll, place the vegetables within the seaweed and roll up the whole thing.

6. Serve with soy sauce and six to eight pieces of sushi. "Bon Appetit"!

CATERPILLAR SUSHI ROLL RECIPE

PREP TIME 30 mins COOK TIME 15 mins.

Ingredients

- 1 Nori sheet
- ⅔ cup of Sushi rice
- 1 Unagi Grilled Eel
- 6 med size Shrimp
- Tempura powder
- Masango

Instructions

1. Grill the eel in the oven for 5 minutes or so.
2. To prepare tempura batter, combine 12 cups of the tempura mix with 12 cups of cold water.
3. Tempura shrimp dipped in a dipping sauce.
4. In the deep fryer, allow to cool on a paper towel.
5. Cover half of a nori sheet with sushi rice.
6. Flip the nori over and spread the shrimp and avocado on top of the nori sheet.
7. Roll it like a sushi roll from the inside out.
8. The roll should be completely covered by thin slices of 1/2 an avocado.
9. Plastic tape should be used to seal the roll. Tighten the avocado to the roll with the sushi rolling mat.
10. Cut the roll into eight pieces by slicing through the plastic tape. Transfer the sushi to a serving platter after removing the tape. Decorate.

LOW-CARB CAULIFLOWER SUSHI

PREP TIME: 40 mins TOTAL TIME: 40 mins

Ingredients

- 500 g (1.1 lb.) raw cauliflower including the stalk cut into chunks.
- 100 g cream cheese full fat
- 1 spring onion thinly sliced.
- 1 tbsp white vinegar
- salt and pepper as need
- vegetables of choice (see recipe notes)
- fish of choice (see recipe notes)
- 4 nori sheets

Instructions

1. Add the raw cauliflower pieces to a food processor fitted with a blade attachment.
2. . Blitz the cauliflower with the blade until it resembles rice.
3. In a food processor, combine all the ingredients until smooth. Blitz the mixture until it's completely incorporated. However, you don't want a purée of either cream cheese or cauliflower.
4. Adjust the ingredients to your liking after tasting the cauliflower rice. People have different preferences when it comes to seasonings.
5. Cream cheese and cauliflower rice combination should be spread out on the nori sheet, leaving 2 inches naked.
6. Stack your veggies, avocado, and salmon in the middle of your plate. The nori sheet should be dampened at the edge, then rolled up securely.
7. Repeat this process with the remaining nori sheets and fillings' Use a sharp, moist knife to cut.
8. Toss with wasabi, soy sauce, or coconut aminos and serve.

CHIRASHI SUSHI CAKE AND TEMARI SUSHI

Prep Time 15 minutes Total Time 15 minutes

Ingredients

- 4 servings cooked Japanese short-grain rice (2 rice-cooker-cups of
- 1 package chirashi sushi mix
- Sakura debut
- kinship tam ago
- 1 Persian/Japanese cucumbers
- For Sushi Cake Decoration
- 10-12 pieces sashimi-grade salmon
- 12 shrimp
- ⅓-½ cup of ikura (salmon roe)
- 2-3 snow peas (blanched, cut diagonally)

Instructions

1. to prepare the sushi known as Chirashi
2. If you want to make pink rice, take away part of the cooked rice and add Sakura debut to it.
3. Add one package of Chirashi Sushi to the remainder of the rice in a big container. Quickly combine when heated. Using a rice paddle, combine all the ingredients into a single dish. Separate the grains of rice using a sharp knife. Make sure it doesn't dry out by covering it with a damp cloth.
4. Make thin crepes out of egg yolks. Cut the remaining egg crepes into thin julienne strips and use 1 egg crepe to make 2 Temari Sushi.
5. For the Chirashi Sushi Cake Assemblage
6. Set up a container that best suits your needs. To begin, lay the egg crepe garnish on the plate. Do not leave any gap between them. Pink rice is next, followed by Chirashi Sushi, which is the last layer. You may embellish the bottom of the container by sprinkling sliced cucumber around the outside of the rice bowl.
7. Dish up and garnish as desired. It's easy to make sashimi rose by placing half a piece over the other and rolling it up.

8. This is a bonus: Temari Sushi Making.
9. Place the thin egg crepe on a sheet of plastic wrap and cut it in half. Wrap the egg crepe firmly with 1-2 Tbsp of Chirashi Sushi on top. When you're ready to serve, keep it in the plastic bag.
10. Place the Temari Sushi on a serving platter when you're ready to serve. Add snow peas, half of the cut shrimp, and ikura to the dish as a final garnish.

CREAM CHEESE AND CRAB SUSHI ROLLS

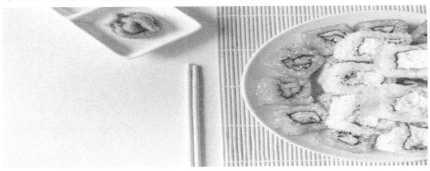

READY IN: 40mins

Ingredients

- 1 cup of white rice
- 1 tsp minced.
- Ginger 2 tbsp
- rice vinegar 1 tsp salt
- 1 cucumber
- Imitation crabmeat, leg style
- Cream cheese
- nori sushi sheet

Instructions

1. Rice and ginger are added to 2 cups of boiling water. It's done when the rice is done cooking and the liquid has evaporated, about 20 minutes.
2. Rice vinegar and salt should be added to the rice, and then stirred in thoroughly.
3. Seaweed sheets are ready to be laid out.
4. Divide the rice into equal halves by wetting your hands.
5. Spread the rice out equally between the two pieces of seaweed.
6. Leave about a half-inch gap between the rice and the bottom of the pan.
7. Toward the top of the pages. I'm going to do something to make the sushi roll even better.
8. faster and less difficult to do.
9. Place the crab on the plate about an inch from the bottom.
10. straight lines of cucumbers with cream cheese
11. both directions at once (left to right).
12. Make sure the sushi is rolled up tightly, yet gently.
13. Avoid ripping the paper as you go from the bottom to the top.
14. Sheets of seaweed
15. Cut the rolls into separate portions using a wet, extremely sharp knife.
16. a variety of sushi dishes

TERIYAKI CHICKEN SUSHI

READY IN: 40mins

Ingredients

- 2 cup of sushi rice
- 1 tbsp rice wine vinegar
- 1 tbsp sugar
- 2 tsp oil
- 400-gram chicken breast fillets, sliced thinly
- 3/4 - 1 cup of teriyaki sauce.
- 6 sheets nori seaweed
- 1 red capsicum thinly sliced.
- 1/2 small cucumber thinly sliced.
-

Instructions

1. You follow the directions on the sushi rice packet. Discard the liquid and set the drained ingredients in a large basin. Set rice aside to cool after adding rice wine vinegar and sugar.

2. Before simmering, heat the oil in a nonstick pan over medium-high heat. Cook for 4 to 5 minutes, or until the chicken is golden brown and well cooked through.

3. Cook the teriyaki sauce until it coats the chicken and has thickened to a syrupy consistency over low heat. Take a break and let it cool.

4. A sushi mat with a glossy side down, place one nori sheet. Gently push the rice into the nori, covering two-thirds of it.

5. Place the chicken, red peppers, and cucumbers in a long strip along the rice. " It may be rolled up with the help of the bamboo mat. Slice the roll in half.

FLOWER CHIRASHI SUSHI

READY IN: 40mins

Ingredients

- Prepare 550 of grams, about 3 small bowlful Plain cooked rice.
- Prepare 1 of commercial Chirashi sushi mix.
- 10 of thin slices Carrot.
- 2 of Dried shiitake mushrooms.
- 1 of Koyi tofu.
- 10 of Mange touts.
- Kinship Tamayo (finely shredded thin omelet).
- 2 of Eggs.
- 1 tsp of Sugar.
- Prawns.
- 5 of to 10 (cooked).
- 1 tbsp of ○Vinegar.
- 1/2 tsp of ○Sugar.
- 1 of Sakura debut.

Instructions

1. Make Kinship Tamayo by adding the ingredients to the eggs.
2. Cutter the carrots into flower-shaped slices. To prepare the dried, thinly sliced shiitake mushrooms, just rehydrate them and slice them.
3. In a dashi broth, cook the Koyi tofu, carrots, and shitake mushrooms (1 cup of dashi stock, 1 tbsp each of sugar, mirin, sake, 1 tsp of acouchi soy sauce and a pinch of salt)..
4. Prepare the prawns by marinating them in the ingredients. When it came to the salad, I used pre-cooked prawns.
5. Cut the Koyi tofu into cubes and place them on a baking sheet. Mix in the chirashi sushi mix, Koyi tofu, and shiitake mushrooms with the rice, and serve!
6. Using a mound, spoon sushi rice into it. When finished, it should look like this.
7. Prawn, carrot, and mange tout slices are arranged on top.
8. Rice that has been refrigerated can be served alongside other ingredients.

FUN FRUIT SUSHI

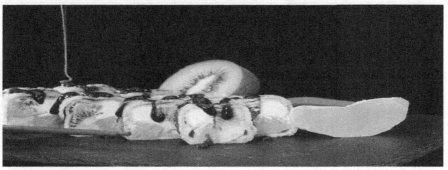

Prep: 10 min Cook: 5 min

Ingredients

- 1 tbsp unsalted butter
- 2/3 cup of mini marshmallows
- 2 cups of cooked rice (any)
- Nonstick vegetable oil spray
- 1 banana thinly sliced.
- 1/2-pint fruit medley, like strawberries, pineapple, kiwi, and cantaloupe

Instructions

1. Using a medium saucepan, melt the butter and marshmallows over medium-low heat until they are fully dissolved. Add cooked rice and stir until fully incorporated.

2. You may use nonstick spray to gently coat the mold or ice cube tray.

3. You'll need to slice the fruit medley into cubes and arrange them in the bottom of the mold. Gently push the rice into the fruit with a spoon.

4. The "sushi" is ready to be unmolded and garnished with toasted coconut and small chocolate chips, as desired.

CHOCOLATE "SUSHI"

Prep Time:45 minutes Wait Time:3 hours.

Ingredients

Modeling Chocolate:

- • 12 oz. semi-sweet chocolate
- • 2 oz. corn syrup
- • 1 cup of rice
- • 2 cups of apple juice
- • Seasonal fruits, julienned.

Instructions

1. The method for making modeling chocolate is as follows: Then add the 2 oz of corn syrup and thoroughly stir the chocolate in a double boiler.
2. Take plastic wrap and cover the mixture. Refrigerate for at least two hours after wrapping in plastic wrap.
3. Slice the julienned fruit into matchstick-sized matchsticks and place them on a baking sheet.
4. Add 1 cup of rice and 2 cups of apple juice to a saucepan and bring to a boil. Bring the mixture to a simmer. Remove from the heat after 5.30 minutes and set aside.
5. Knead the other half of the modeling chocolate until it is flexible and ready to use. Roll out a sheet of paper as thin as possible. If the surface is too rough, simply run your palm over it.
6. Modeling chocolate may be cut into 2-1/2-inch broad strips.
7. A seam should be left on the side where sticky rice is placed on the chocolate. Decorate with fruit and rice.
8. As you roll, be careful to secure the ends with tape.
9. To harden, put in the fridge. The remaining modeling chocolate can be used in the same manner.
10. Cut your rolls into one-inch lengths with a sharp knife. Garnish your meal with this item.

NUTELLA AND BANANA SUSHI

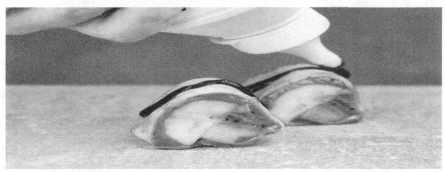

Prep Time:45 minutes Wait Time:3 hours.

Ingredients

Modeling Chocolate:
- 2 tortillas
- 4 tbs Nutella chocolate hazelnut spread.
- 2 bananas

Instructions

1. Spread Nutella on a piece of bread before cutting.
2. Peel a banana and place it on the tortilla's edge, then roll it up.
3. Wrap a tortilla around a banana.
4. Make circles out of the slices and place them on a dish, cut side up.

MAKING CLASSIC CALIFORNIA ROLLS IS EASIER THAN YOU THINK

Ingredients

- game Sushi Nori Sheets
- sushi rice
- water
- vinegar
- fine sea salt
- toasted sesame seeds
- imitation crab meat, shredded.
- mayonnaise
- sugar
- English cucumber
- avocado

Instructions

1. Drain the rice completely after rinsing in cold water until the water runs clear.

2. In a pot, combine all the rice and water and set to the boil. Take a pot and bring it to a boil, then lower the heat and simmer for 18 to 23 minutes, or until the rice is done.

3. Add 2 Tbsp rice vinegar and 2 Tbsp of sea salt to the cooked rice in a large mixing bowl, then fold the mixture often just before it reaches room temperature.

4. During this time, prepare the veggies and the crab salad. Cut the avocado and cucumber into thin sticks once they have been sliced.

5. Shred the crab in a food processor, then add the mayonnaise, rice vinegar, and sugar and blend until combined.

6. It's now or never! Place the sushi mat so that the long sticks run horizontally across your work surface, with the mat facing you. Using damp hands, evenly spread 14 – 12 inch of chilled sushi rice over 1 sheet of Sushi Nori, rough side up, on a mat.

7. Turn over the Sushi Nori mat and sprinkle the rice with 12 tsp of toasted sesame seeds.
8. Spread about 3 Tbsp crab salad over the width of the Sushi Nori, about an inch from the Sushi Nori/rice border closest to you.
9. Slices of avocado and cucumber can be arranged in rows in front of the crab.
10. Now is the time to begin rolling the sushi, so get to work. Use your fingers to keep the components in place while you wrap up the sushi-like a burrito. When you're done rolling, lift the sushi mat off the tucked piece and continue to do so.
11. Removing the mat is as simple as rolling it up and throwing it away. Make eight slices of sushi using a damp serrated knife. When cutting sticky rice, use a damp knife. To produce eight bite-sized pieces, follow this tip: cut your sushi roll in half lengthwise, then in half again widthwise.

NUTELLA AND BANANA SUSHI

Prep Time:45 minutes Wait Time:3 hours.

Ingredients

- 2 tortillas
- 4 tbs Nutella chocolate hazelnut spread.
- 2 bananas

Instructions

1. Spread Nutella on a piece of bread before cutting.
2. Peel a banana and place it on the tortilla's edge, then roll it up.
3. Wrap a tortilla around a banana.
4. Make circles out of the slices and place them on a dish, cut side up.

COCONUT FRUSHI

Prep Time:45 minutes Wait Time:3 hours.

Ingredients

- 1 1/4 cups of water
- 1 cup of sushi rice
- 1/4 cup of sugar
- 1/4 cup of coconut milk (canned, not fresh)
- cooking spray
- 10 mandarin orange slices from a can (drained)
- 10 raspberries, cut in half.
- Optional: vanilla yogurt for dipping

Instructions

1. A pot of water and rice should be brought to the point of boiling. Simmer for 15 minutes with lid on and heat reduced to low. Take the rice out of the pot, cover it, and let it rest for about 15 minutes.

2. Gently combine rice, sugar, and coconut milk in a large bowl. Wait for 20 minutes before removing the lid.

3. Spray some cooking spray on your hands. Make 20 equal-sized rice balls and shape them into an oval shape. To get the desired form, you may alternatively use an oval-shaped tbsp. As you shape them, push and squeeze the rice to keep it in one piece.

4. One orange slice or two raspberry halves should be placed on top of each one.

5. If preferred, serve with a side of vanilla yogurt for dipping.

BEEFY CALI ROLL

Ingredients

Hand vinegar:
- 1 cup of water
- ¼ cup of rice vinegar
- Piquant Sauce:
- ½ cup of plain yogurt
- 1 tbsp mustard
- 1 tbsp horseradish
- ½ avocado, mashed until smooth

Maki:
- 2 sheets nori
- 2 cups of prepared sushi rice
- 6 thin slices corned beef.
- ½ avocado, cut into slivers
- ¼ cucumber, cut lengthwise into thin strips

Toppings:
- Chopped chives.
- Wasabi peas, for serving.

Instructions

1. Set away the hand vinegar in a small bowl until it is time to make use of it.
2. Blend the yogurt, mustard, horseradish, and avocado in a small bowl to make the sauce.
3. Place a sushi mat made of bamboo on a dry, clean surface. Use hand vinegar to dampen hands and brush off any excess that may have fallen on them. Shiny side down, place a nori sheet. Leave 1 inch of nori vacant at the farthest end from you when spreading half the rice on it.
4. The rice should be covered in half of the corned beef, avocado and cucumber that is closest to you.
5. Securing the filling with your fingers, use your thumbs to press up the nori mat just before it touches the rice on one side. Afterward, you may fold it in half. Make sure you're firmly pressing down on the roll.
6. Rolled tightly and round, lift up the mat's top. Shape the roll by gently squeezing it. The rice should be firmly pressed in at the ends to prevent it from spilling out. Remove the bamboo mat and put the roll in a safe place to be used another time.
7. It's the same process for the second roll. Cut each roll into eight slices with a very thin, sharp knife. Sprinkle each piece with chopped chives and a few wasabi peas on a sushi dish. Make a spicy sauce to go with it.

KETO CALIFORNIA ROLL STUFFED AVOCADO

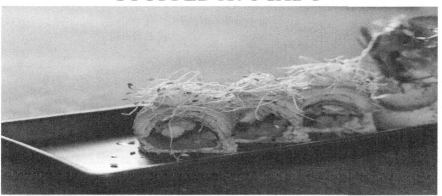

Ingredients

- 2 tbsp unsalted butter
- 2 tbsp flour
- 2 green onions, with about 2 inches green, thinly sliced.
- 1 tsp chopped fresh parsley.
- 1/4 cup of dry sherry
- 4 ounces lump crabmeat
- 2 cups of heavy whipping cream
- 1 1/2 tsp Cajun seasoning, or Creole seasoning, or as need.
- 1 tbsp tomato paste
- Salt, as need
- Freshly ground black pepper, as need

Instructions

1. Melt the butter in a big saucepan over low heat; add the flour, onion, and parsley and mix until smooth. Cook for 5 minutes, stirring often.
2. Crabmeat and sherry should be added gradually to the flour mixture while being stirred continually. Add Cajun spice and tomato paste to the mixture. Simmer for around 5 minutes to slightly thicken the sauce and make it a little less watery.
3. If preferred, add salt and pepper to you taste.
4. Enjoy.

SHERRY CREAM CRAB SAUCE

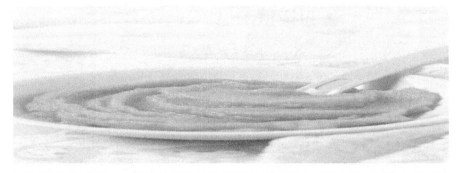

Prep: 10 mins Cook: 10 mins Total: 20 mins

Ingredients

- 6 oz good quality crab meat (egg canned claw meat)
- 2 tbs mayonnaise
- salt and black pepper
- wasabi paste, as need, optional
- hot sauce, optional plating garnish
- 1 ripe but firm avocado
- ¼ cup of diced English cucumber
- ¼ tsp sesame seeds, to garnish
- 2 tsp tobiko (flying fish roe), to garnish

Instructions

1. Crab, mayonnaise, salt, pepper, and wasabi paste are combined in a bowl (if using).
2. Spread lines of hot sauce on a tiny serving dish with a drizzle bottle for a slick presentation.
3. By slicing the avocado in half lengthwise, you can get rid of the pit. Allow each avocado half to stand on its own by cutting a small piece from the bottom.
4. Crab mixture should be divided between avocado halves by filling the cavity first and then sprinkling it on top.
5. Finish with a tablespoon of tobiko and a sprinkling of cucumber and sesame seeds.

PHILADELPHIA ROLL

Ingredients

- 2 cups of sushi rice (460 g)
- ¼ cup of seasoned rice vinegar (60 mL)
- 4 half sheets sushi-grade nori
- 4 oz smoked salmon (115 g)
- 4 oz cream cheese (115 g), cut into matchsticks.
- 1 small cucumber, cut into matchsticks.

Instructions

1. Rice vinegar should be sprayed over the sushi rice, fanning and tossing until the rice is at room temperature.
2. On the rolling mat, the nori should be put out so that the rough side is facing up.
3. Grab a handful of rice and lay it on the nori with your wet hands. Use a spatula to spread the rice evenly on the nori sheet without squashing it.
4. Place smoked salmon, cream cheese, and cucumber in a horizontal row 1 inch from the bottom.
5. To construct a tight roll, grab both nori sheets and a mat and roll them over the filling until the additional space at the bottom hits the opposite side. Maintain the roll's form by squeezing it as you go.
6. A cutting board should be used to transfer the roll. After rubbing the knife on a wet paper towel, cut the roll into six equal pieces.
7. Enjoy!

CALIFORNIA ROLLS

Prep: 50 min Cook: 25 min

Ingredients

- 3 1/3 cups of rice
- 5 1/3 tbsp vinegar
- 5 tbsp sugar
- 3 tbsp salt
- 10 sheets seaweed, halved.
- 1/2-pound imitation crab
- 1/4 cup of mayonnaise
- 1 cucumber, peeled, seeded, and julienne.
- 1 avocado, peeled, seeded.
- Sesame seeds

Instructions

1. Rinse the rice thoroughly until it is free of any debris. Allow the rice to sit for 30 minutes after draining it in a colander. Using a rice cooker or pot, add 4 cups of water or follow the manufacturer's directions. A boil should be achieved. Stir occasionally and bring to a simmer before covering. Toss in the vegetables and let them cook for about 15 minutes. Remove the lid, throw a moist cloth over the rice, and let it to cool for 10 minutes before serving.

2. Sushi vinegar can be purchased pre-made or produced at home by boiling vinegar, sugar, and salt in a pot until the sugar and salt dissolve. Sweeter vinegar may be made by simply adding additional sugar.

3. Gently combine cooked rice with sushi vinegar. Turn off your rice cooker and pour the vinegar into a wooden bowl for making sushi rice. The vinegar can also be added to a rice cooker and mixed thoroughly before being allowed to cool to room temperature. As a result, leaving the lid open is the best option.

4. Using plastic wrap, cover a sushi rolling mat (makisu). Place a half-sheet of seaweed on the mat and press it firmly into place. Distribute

a small amount of rice evenly over the seaweed. In a small bowl, combine the imitation crab and mayonnaise. Gather the rice around a portion of the imitation crab flesh meat. Stack rice with a layer of cucumber and avocado in the middle. Using a mat and plastic wrap, roll the rice around the filling and then press softly to seal it in. Spray some sesame seeds on it once you take off the baking mat and plastic wrap. Cut the sushi into bite-sized pieces. Repeat with the rest of the ingredients.

SPICY CRAB ROLL RECIPE

Prep Time: 15 minutes Cook Time: 45 minutes. Total Time: 1 hour

Ingredients

For Sushi Rice

- 1 cup of sushi rice short-grain sushi rice
- 1 cup of water
- 1 ½ tbsp sushi vinegar (or mix 1 tbsp rice vinegar, 1/2 tbsp sugar, and 1/2 tsp salt)
- Spicy Mayo
- 3 tsp mayonnaise
- 1 ½ tsp sriracha sauce

For the Spicy Kane Roll

- 4 oz Kane crab meat
- 2 sheets nori seaweed
- 2 tbsp sesame seeds

Instructions

1. Add the rice to the rice cooker once it has been rinsed. Then, add water and follow the recipe.
2. Once the food has cooled, put it to a big bowl. Pour sushi vinegar into the mixture while it's still lukewarm (or the mixture of rice vinegar, sugar and salt).
3. Mayo with a kick of sriracha
4. Mix Sriracha sauce and mayonnaise in a transparent dish. If you like a hotter taste, add additional Sriracha to the mix.
5. The recipe for a spicy crab salad may be found here:
6. Hands or two forks can be used to shred the fake crab flesh.
7. Then, add Sriracha mayonnaise and thoroughly combine.
8. Make the Spicy Crab Roll now.
9. Kitchen scissors may be used to divide the nori sheet in half.
10. Make sure the glossy side of the nori sheet is facing down when you place it on the bamboo mat.
11. Spread about 3/4 cup of seasoned sushi rice equally over the nori. Gently knead the rice with your fingertips. You can use Tezu water to keep the rice from sticking to your hands.

12. Top the rice with sesame seeds.
13. Turn the sheet over so that the rice-facing side is on the bottom.
14. Serve with some hot Kani crab salad on top.
15. Using your thumbs, raise the bamboo mat's edge up and over the stuffing.
16. Press the rice and filling into the bamboo mat as you roll it away from you. Keep traveling till you reach your destination.
17. Cut the roll into eight equal halves on a cutting board.
18. To ramp up the spiciness, top the roll with more spicy mayo sauce.

SPICY SUSHI ROLL

Prep:15 mins Total:15 mins

Ingredients

- ¼ cup of mayonnaise
- 1 tbsp Chile sauce
- 1 ½ tsp togarashi (Japanese seven spice)
- 1 tsp prepared wasabi
- 1 tsp chili powder
- 1 tsp paprika
- 3 (3 ounce) fillets imitation crab meat, cut into 1 1/2-inch pieces
- 2 cups of cooked sushi rice
- 3 sheets nori (dry seaweed)

Instructions

1. Chili sauce and mayonnaise are combined in a bowl; add imitation crab meat and mix until it's equally covered.

2. Each nori sheet should have a uniform coating of rice spread across it. Each nori sheet should have a layer of crabmeat mixture spooned along the top edge. Using a nori sheet, wrap the crabmeat mixture filling around the nori sheet, starting from the filling side. Cut each roll into eight equal halves.

HOMEMADE PHILADELPHIA ROLL

Prep time 15 minutes cook time 2 minutes.

Ingredients

- 3-4 oz raw sashimi-grade or lightly smoked salmon
- 1/2 cup of sushi rice
- 2 TBSP seasoned rice vinegar
- 1 sheet of nori seaweed
- 2 oz cream cheese or as need.
- 1-2 tsp toasted sesame seeds
- Sriracha chili sauce and/or soy sauce for dipping

Instructions

1. Use a mesh strainer to thoroughly rinse half a cup of of sushi rice in cold water. To drain, shake the strainer vigorously until the water is clear and the strainer is no longer wet.

2. A medium saucepan should be filled with rice and 2/3 cup of cold water, and the heat should be turned up to high. Add water and bring it to a boil, then lower the heat and cover it. Add another ten minutes of steaming time after the 20 minutes of cooking covered.

3. Fluff with a fork in a non-metallic basin. Mix with 2 tablespoons of seasoned rice vinegar. Take a break from the rest of your sushi preparations to chill down the eel.

4. The cold cream cheese may be rolled or shaped into ropes long enough to distribute horizontally over your seaweed sheet. Set away for later.

5. Take a knife and cut the fish into thin slices. Adding scallions and/or cucumber as an optional garnish (or both, because they're so good in any combination!) Preparation for them is also required. Cucumber matchsticks and scallions are two of my favorite ingredients.

6. After that, layout a bamboo mat covered in plastic wrap and top it with nori.

7. Turn the seaweed sheet so that the rectangle is vertical/tall and thinly spread rice over it. Top with seaweed and rice for an outward appearance of seaweed on the exterior. Flip your nori sheet so that the rice touches the plastic-wrapped mat and lay filling straight on the nori for rice on the outside with filling within.

8. Place sliced salmon, cream cheese, and any vegetables in a horizontal row about an inch from the bottom of your rice.

9. Unfold the bamboo mat after rolling about a quarter of the mat over the filling and gently squeezing (so that it clings to the rice underneath it). Assemble a spiral by rolling a sheet of rice and seaweed together with vegetables. It's time to give it a final push to close the deal. Click here for a step-by-step pictorial guide to the procedure.

10. Make six bite-sized discs out of each roll using a chef's knife that has just been sharpened. Sesame seeds and soy sauce or Sriracha chili sauce can be sprinkled on the sliced side.

SMOKED SALMON & AVOCADO HAND ROLLS

Prep:10 mins Total:10 mins

Ingredients

- ¼ avocado, mashed
- 3 nori (seaweed) sheets
- ¾ cup of cooked and cooled brown rice
- 1 (1-ounce) sliced smoked salmon
- 3 tomato slices
- 3 tbsp chopped red onion.
- 1 tbsp capers

Instructions

1. Spread nori sheets with avocado.
2. Salmon, brown rice and arugula on top of the avocado; nori sheets rolled up. Use a serrated knife to cut rolls into pieces.

NIGIRI SUSHI WITH AVOCADO, CUCUMBER, AND SHISO LEAVES

Prep:10 mins Total:10 mins

Ingredients

- Sushi rice
- 11/2 cups of short-grain white rice
- 1 Tbs.'s sake
- 21/2 Tbs. rice vinegar
- 11/2 tsp. sugar
- 3/4 tsp. salt
-
- Topping
- 1 tsp. prepared wasabi, or more as needed.
- 24 thin avocado slices (3/4 of an avocado)
- 24 paper-thin English cucumber half-moon slices (1/4 cucumber)
- 12 shiso leaves, halved diagonally.

Instructions

1. Making sushi rice: Using a strainer, remove any remaining starch from the rice. Add 1⅔ cups of cold water and sake to a pot and bring to a boil. Increase heat to medium-high, bring to a boil, then reduce to low. Simmer for 10 minutes, covered. Cover and allow sit for another 10 minutes before serving.

2. In a bowl, combine vinegar, sugar, and salt and whisk until well combined. Rice should now be placed in a big bowl, with half of its vinegar mixture drizzled over it. Continue to pour vinegar mixture and cut through rice until all vinegar mixture is absorbed, then take the rice from the pot. Cool by covering with a wet towel.

3. Shape 2 Tbs of Sushi Rice into a two-bite-sized oval using damp palms. Top the rice with a dab of wasabi and two avocado and two cucumber slices. Stack veggies on top of half of a shiso leaf with the middle seam horizontally. Repeat this process with the remaining rice and toppings. ' With soy sauce on the side.

KAPPAMAKI (CUCUMBER SUSHI ROLL)

Prep:20 mins Cook:0 mins Total:20 mins

Ingredients

- 4 sheets nori, cut in half.
- 6 cups of prepared sushi rice
- 2 Japanese cucumbers, cut into long sticks.

Instructions

1. Organize the components.
2. Put a slice of nori on top of a bamboo mat (makisu) (makisu).
3. Spread approximately 3/4 cup Ogushi rice on top of the nori sheets.
4. Stack one-eighth of an inch of cucumber on top of the rice.
5. Sushi is rolled up in a cylinder by rolling the bamboo mat up and pressing forward.
6. With both hands, firmly press down on the bamboo mat.
7. Remove the sushi roll off the bamboo mat by unwrapping it. Make more rolls by repeating the procedure.
8. Before cutting sushi, dampen a knife with water and let it dry completely.
9. Slice the sushi roll into small pieces.

VEGAN DECONSTRUCTED SUSHI SALAD BOWL WITH SESAME GINGER MISO DRESSING

PREP TIME 10 mins TOTAL TIME 10 mins

Ingredients

- Salad Bowl:
- 4 cups of chopped baby spinach
- ⅔ cup of cooked brown rice I thawed frozen brown rice
- 1 ½ cup of shelled edamame I thawed frozen edamame.
- ½ English cucumber sliced into strips
- ½ cup of shredded carrots
- 8-10 seaweed snacks or nori
- ½ avocado sliced
- 2 tbsp hemp seeds or sesame seeds
- Sesame Ginger Miso Dressing:

- 1 tbsp miso
- 2 tbsp warm water
- 1 tbsp toasted sesame oil
- 1 tbsp apple cider vinegar
- 1 tsp fresh grated ginger
- 1 tsp maple syrup optional

Instructions

1. Mix in a handful of spinach into each bowl and top with portions of brown rice, seaweed, and avocado. Top with hemp seeds.

2. Mix miso and water with a fork in a small bowl until well combined. Mix in the other ingredients until well-combined. Serve with salads drizzled with the dressing. If you are preparing salad ahead of time or for takeaway, it is better to keep the dressing separate before you are ready to eat.

FRIED SUSHI ROLLS

PREP TIME 10 mins TOTAL TIME 10 mins

Ingredients

- 2 cups of sushi rice (cooked)
- 4 dried seaweed sheets
- ½ cup of mirin
- ½ cup of soy sauce
- 1 tbsp sugar
- 1 cucumber
- 1 avocado
- 9 oz salmon fillets
- 1 sweet potato
- 2 tbsp wasabi paste.
- 6 flours
- 2 eggs
- 6 tbsp panko breadcrumbs
- ¾ cup of vegetable oil

Instructions

1. Using a small saucepan, combine mirin, soy sauce, sugar, and water and bring to a boil over medium heat. Simmer until the sauce thickens. Stop cooking and allow to cool.

2. Cut cucumber into matchsticks after quartering and deseeding. After halves and pitting, thinly slice the avocado's flesh. It's time to slice up some fish! Take a sushi mat and cut the dried seaweed sheets in half lengthwise. Sweet potatoes should be peeled, sliced into thin strips, and then fried until tender.

3. Spread the sushi rice evenly on the seaweed sheet with wet fingertips. Make sure the sushi rice is covered in wasabi paste in the middle. For a vegetarian option, use avocado and sweet potato; for a salmon and cucumber wrap, use the same ingredients.

4. Using the sushi mat, form a tight roll. Set out deep dishes or bowls for each of the three ingredients. Flour first, then egg, and finally panko, dredge the sushi rolls.

5. The sushi rolls should be fried in vegetable oil in a large frying pan before they are browned on both sides.

6. Make a netsuke sauce drizzling over the fried buns. Use wasabi sauce and wasabi ginger as a condiment for the rice and other dishes. Enjoy!

109

GRILLED BACON SUSHI ROLL

Prep: 15 mins Cook: 35 mins Total: 50 mins

Ingredients

- Six thick slices bacon
- ½ pound lean ground beef
- 1 tbsp barbeque spice rub, or as need.
- 4 thin slices prosciutto
- 2 jalapeno peppers, sliced into long strips.
- 2 sticks pepper Jack cheese
- 2 tbsp barbeque sauce, or as need.
- 1 cup of French-fried onions

Instructions

1. On a sushi mat, lay down two strips of bacon, one on top of the other, facing lengthwise.

2. Ground beef and spice rub should be combined in a big dish for the best flavor and texture. You'll need to leave about an inch of bacon exposed on one end of the bacon for this method to work. Cover the meat with prosciutto. Sprinkle the end nearest to you with jalapenos. Place jalapeño strips and cheese sticks next to each other.

3. The exposed end of the bacon should be neatly rolled up.

4. Prepare the grill for 350 degrees Fahrenheit (175 degrees C). Cook the bacon roll, seam side down, for about 25 minutes over indirect heat. Apply a thin layer of barbecue sauce over the top. Grill for another 5 minutes or so, or until the sauce is coated. Grill for a further 5 minutes with the remaining barbecue sauce on top, then serve.

5. Using a spatula, spread the fried onions evenly over the meat. With chopsticks, cut and serve the meat.

CHICKEN KARAAGE SUSHI

PREP TIME 30 mins COOK TIME 35 mins. TOTAL TIME 1 hr 5 mins

Ingredients

For the sushi rice

- 1 cup of short
- ¼ cup of rice vinegar
- 1 tbsp caster sugar
- ½ tsp salt

For the rolling and filling

- 3 sheets nori
- ½ cucumber in matchsticks
- Superb Herb garlic chives
- 1 carrot peeled.

For the chicken karaage

- ½ box Diamond
- 2 Chicken Thigh Fillets quartered.
- 2 cups of Oliva do Avocado Cooking Oil for deep frying
- serve with
- pickled ginger
- wasabi
- soy Sauce

Instructions

1. To make sushi rice, follow the directions on the rice packet.
2. For the karaage, use the following: Coat 'n Cook chicken thighs with the seasoning mixture. Fully cover each piece in the spicy crumb.
3. In a heavy-bottomed pan or wok, heat the oil to medium-high (170°C). Chicken pieces are added to the oil with tongs, frying until they are golden brown and cooked through (about 5 minutes). Layout on a paper towel-lined rack to dry Make sure you do this with all of the pieces.
4. Sushi rice should be prepared according to the instructions on the box., then spread it out evenly over the seaweed on the bamboo mat.
5. Rice should be topped with a layer of chicken karaage, carrots, cucumbers, and garlic chives. It's time to tuck it in. Continually repeat this method with the remaining of the components.
6. Serve with pickled ginger, wasabi, and soy sauce, if desired, after cutting the sushi into rounds with a sharp knife. Yum!

SPICY TUNA ROLL

PREP TIME:30 mins TOTAL TIME:30 mins

Ingredients

- 1 ½ cup of sushi rice (cooked and seasoned) (each roll requires ¾ cup of (135 g) sushi rice. 1 rice cooker cup of (180 ml /150 g) makes 330 g (12 oz, 1 ¾ cup of) of cooked rice.)
- 4 oz sashimi-grade tuna
- 3 tsp sriracha sauce
- ½ tsp roasted sesame oil
- 2 green onions/ scallions (cut into thin rounds)
- 1 sheet nori (seaweed) (each roll requires half sheet; cut in half crosswise)
- 2 tbsp toasted white sesame seeds.

Instructions

1. Gather all the necessary supplies. Sushi rice manufacturing time is not included in the cooking time. Please refer to the sushi rice recipe for a detailed instruction to making sushi rice. To keep the sushi rice from drying out, always use a moist towel to cover it. Apply a layer of plastic wrap on your bamboo sushi mat.
2. In a small dish, combine 14 cup (4 Tbsp) of water and 2 tsp rice vinegar and mix well. Rice does not adhere to your fingers when you dip them in water.
3. Cube the tuna into 14-inch cubes (0.5 cm) (or you can mince the tuna).
4. Toss the tuna, Sriracha sauce, sesame oil, and a few green onions together in a medium-sized dish before serving (save some for topping).
5. On the bamboo mat, place a half-sheet of nori with the glossy side facing up. Spread 34 cups of rice out evenly on the nori sheet using Tezu-wet fingertips. Sesame seeds can be sprinkled over the rice.

- spicy mayo
- For Vinegar Water for Dipping Fingers.
- ¼ cup of water (4 Tbsp)
- 2 tsp rice vinegar

112

6. It's time for the rice to face down on the nori sheet! Nori sheet should be placed at the bottom of the bamboo mat. Spread out half of the tuna mixture on the nori sheet, starting at the bottom.
7. Keep the contents in place with your fingertips as you wrap the bamboo mat into a cylinder. Roll the bamboo mat forward while maintaining a moderate pressure on the surface of the mat.
8. Cut the roll in half, then into three equal halves using a sharp knife. Use tegu or plastic wrap to keep the rice from sticking to your fingers when cutting sushi rolls.
9. Use the leftover green onion to garnish each sushi roll with a dab of spicy mayonnaise.

EASY SHRIMP SUSHI

Prep Time: 40 min Cook Time: 20 min. Total Time: 1 hour

Ingredients

- 1 cup of uncooked sushi rice
- 8 raw large shrimp shelled and deveined.
- 1 tbsp butter
- 1 tbsp rice vinegar
- 1 clove garlic, crushed.
- 1 cucumber, cut into thin strips.
- 1 avocado sliced thin.
- 5 sheets roasted seaweed papers.
- Soy sauce and wasabi for dipping

Instructions

1. Uncooked rice and 2 cups of water should be placed in a Rice Cooker to begin the process of cooking. The rice used for sushi is short grain and extremely sticky. If you want to cook on the stove, then follow the package instructions.
2. The butter and garlic should be heated in a small pot while the rice cooks. Add the prawns after the garlic has begun to smell.
3. Take care to cook the shrimp to a pinkish color. Before serving, remove the shrimp from the pan and slice them into little pieces.
4. Toss in the rice vinegar once it's cooked and swirl to combine.
5. Add shrimp, avocado, and cucumber to the bottom third of the seaweed sheet, then spread the remaining rice on top.
6. Slice everything into little pieces. Continually repeat this procedure with the remaining components.
7. Sauces such as soy sauce and wasabi can be served alongside.

DRAGON ROLL

PREP TIME:1 hr. TOTAL TIME:1 hr.

Ingredients

- 1 Persian/Japanese cucumbers (4 oz, 113 g)
- 2 avocados (12 oz, 340 g)
- ½ lemon (optional)
- 2 sheets nori (seaweed) (cut in half crosswise)
- 2 cups of sushi rice (cooked and seasoned) (each roll needs ½ cup of (90 g) sushi rice)
- 8 pieces shrimp tempura
- 2 Tbsp tobiko (flying fish roe)
- unagi (eel) (optional)
- For toppings
- spicy mayo
- unagi sauce
- toasted black sesame seeds.
- Vinegar water for

Instructions

1. Gather all of the necessary supplies.
2. Cucumbers may be cut into quarters by cutting them lengthwise. After removing the seeds, split each half lengthwise in two.
3. After slicing it in half lengthwise, take care not to damage the seed when twisting the pieces apart. Cut into the pit using the knife's blade. Twist the skin of the avocado in the opposite way with the other hand. A seamless exit from the pit is guaranteed.
4. Take the avocado's peel, then slice it in half horizontally.
5. After pushing lightly with your fingertips, keep pressing with the side of your knife until the length of avocado slices is about as long as a sushi roll's (length of nori seaweed). Squeezing lemon over the avocado will avoid discoloration if the sushi roll isn't served immediately away.
6. A nori sheet, shiny side down, is placed on the bamboo mat covered with plastic wrap. Spread half a cup of sushi rice on the nori sheet by dipping your hands in tegu (vinegar water).

dipping hands (tegu)
- ¼ cup of water
- 2 tsp rice vinegar

7. Put the tempura shrimp, cucumber strips, and tobiko at the bottom of the nori sheet and flip it over to serve. Unagi can also be added to this dish if desired.
8. Roll the nori sheet tightly and firmly over the filled with bamboo mat from the bottom end until the nori sheet reaches the bottom end. Lift the bamboo mat and roll on top of yourself.
9. Make sure the roll is securely squeezed by placing the bamboo mat over the roll.
10. The avocado should be placed on top of the roll with the side of the knife.
11. Place the bamboo mat on top of the roll and cover with plastic wrap. Squeeze the sushi roll until the avocado slices completely encircle the sushi. Tighten the roll. Avoid breaking the avocado slices by being careful.
12. With a knife, cut the roll into eight equal pieces. Use a moist cloth to wipe off the blade after each use. The bamboo mat may be used to re-squeeze the sushi roll if it gets messed up when cutting. The sushi should be served on a serving platter once the plastic wrap is removed.
13. Sprinkle black sesame seeds and a dollop of spicy mayo over each piece of sushi before adding the tobiko. Put some unagi sauce on the dish if you'd like to dip your sushi in it.
14. Enjoy!

DRAGON SUSHI ROLL

Ingredients

- Sushi Rice see recipe.
- 2 sheets nori
- 1 cucumber
- 2 avocados
- 2 tbsp caviar
- 1 lemon
- 8 tempura or panko prawns' shop-boughten click on the link in notes below
- For Toppings
- Kewpie Japanese Mayo shop
- Fused Cheeky Chili Soy Sauce shop.
- 2 tbsp sesame seeds
- Caviar recommend Goats bridge.

Instructions

1. Preparation of the sushi mat
2. Using clingfilm, cover a sushi mat to keep the rice from clinging to it. You'll need a clean moist towel and a small dish of water while you're rolling the sushi.
3. If you're using a sushi mat without clingfilm, place half a sheet of nori shining side down, with the nori's lines running vertically. A quarter of the sushi rice should be placed on the nori (100g). Rice and sesame seeds or furikake can be sprinkled over the nori sheet using lightly wet hands.
4. Using a second sushi mat, carefully push it down on top of the first to hold the rice in place. Remove the top sushi mat by flipping the mats over so that the mat that was facing up is now facing down. If you have rice on top of nori, you're good to go! Take a break from preparing the fillings while you do this.
5. To make the avocado and sushi fillings:
6. Remove the seeds by halving the cucumber and cutting it in half. To have 8 pieces, cut each half-length into four pieces.
7. Scoop out the avocado half with a spoon, then use a sharp knife to thinly slice the avocado in half. To prevent the avocado from becoming

brown, sprinkle it with a little lemon juice. Place a sharp knife against the avocado slices and gently press until the slices are the length of the sushi roll. Remove the avocado from the knife.

8. Place the prawns, cucumbers, and caviar in a straight line on the nori sheet, then fold the nori in half. The closest end of the mat should be held by your index and thumb fingers. To keep the ingredients in place, you'll need to use the rest of your hands. Roll the nori and rice wrap around the contents. Make a roll by pressing down firmly but gently.

9. It's best not to worry if there are any components that have escaped from each side of the roll; simply press them back in and don't worry about the roll being messy. Wrap the sushi mat around the sushi roll to keep it in place and prevent it from unraveling.

10. Your sharp knife may be used to place avocado slices on top of your sushi rolls.

11. Wrap the sushi roll in clingfilm, then cover it with a bamboo mat. Squeeze the roll gently until the avocado slices around the fish.

12. Cut the clingfilm-wrapped roll in half with a sharp knife on a chopping board. Using a moist towel, wipe the knife clean and cut each piece in half until you have eight. Remove the cling film before serving.

13. In the same manner, make three more rolls of dough.

14. Top the sushi roll with caviar, sesame seeds, and a spicy mayo sauce before serving.

DRAGON SUSHI ROLL

Ingredients

- Sushi Rice see recipe.
- 2 sheets nori
- 1 cucumber
- 2 avocados
- 2 tbsp caviar
- 1 lemon
- 8 tempura or panko prawns' shop-boughten click on the link in notes below
- For Toppings
- Kewpie Japanese Mayo shop
- Fused Cheeky Chili Soy Sauce shop.
- 2 tbsp sesame seeds
- Caviar recommend Goats bridge.

Instructions

1. Preparation of the sushi mat
2. Using clingfilm, cover a sushi mat to keep the rice from clinging to it. You'll need a clean moist towel and a small dish of water while you're rolling the sushi.
3. If you're using a sushi mat without clingfilm, place half a sheet of nori shining side down, with the nori's lines running vertically. A quarter of the sushi rice should be placed on the nori (100g). Rice and sesame seeds or furikake can be sprinkled over the nori sheet using lightly wet hands.
4. Using a second sushi mat, carefully push it down on top of the first to hold the rice in place. Remove the top sushi mat by flipping the mats over so that the mat that was facing up is now facing down. If you have rice on top of nori, you're good to go! Take a break from preparing the fillings while you do this.
5. To make the avocado and sushi fillings:
6. Remove the seeds by halving the cucumber and cutting it in half. To have 8 pieces, cut each half-length into four pieces.
7. Scoop out the avocado half with a spoon, then use a sharp knife to thinly slice the avocado in half. To prevent the avocado from becoming

DRAGON SUSHI ROLL

Ingredients

- Sushi Rice see recipe.
- 2 sheets nori
- 1 cucumber
- 2 avocados
- 2 tbsp caviar
- 1 lemon
- 8 tempura or panko prawns' shop-boughten click on the link in notes below
- For Toppings
- Kewpie Japanese Mayo shop
- Fused Cheeky Chili Soy Sauce shop.
- 2 tbsp sesame seeds
- Caviar recommend Goats bridge.

Instructions

1. Preparation of the sushi mat
2. Using clingfilm, cover a sushi mat to keep the rice from clinging to it. You'll need a clean moist towel and a small dish of water while you're rolling the sushi.
3. If you're using a sushi mat without clingfilm, place half a sheet of nori shining side down, with the nori's lines running vertically. A quarter of the sushi rice should be placed on the nori (100g). Rice and sesame seeds or furikake can be sprinkled over the nori sheet using lightly wet hands.
4. Using a second sushi mat, carefully push it down on top of the first to hold the rice in place. Remove the top sushi mat by flipping the mats over so that the mat that was facing up is now facing down. If you have rice on top of nori, you're good to go! Take a break from preparing the fillings while you do this.
5. To make the avocado and sushi fillings:
6. Remove the seeds by halving the cucumber and cutting it in half. To have 8 pieces, cut each half-length into four pieces.
7. Scoop out the avocado half with a spoon, then use a sharp knife to thinly slice the avocado in half. To prevent the avocado from becoming

brown, sprinkle it with a little lemon juice. Place a sharp knife against the avocado slices and gently press until the slices are the length of the sushi roll. Remove the avocado from the knife.

8. Place the prawns, cucumbers, and caviar in a straight line on the nori sheet, then fold the nori in half. The closest end of the mat should be held by your index and thumb fingers. To keep the ingredients in place, you'll need to use the rest of your hands. Roll the nori and rice wrap around the contents. Make a roll by pressing down firmly but gently.

9. It's best not to worry if there are any components that have escaped from each side of the roll; simply press them back in and don't worry about the roll being messy. Wrap the sushi mat around the sushi roll to keep it in place and prevent it from unraveling.

10. Your sharp knife may be used to place avocado slices on top of your sushi rolls.

11. Wrap the sushi roll in clingfilm, then cover it with a bamboo mat. Squeeze the roll gently until the avocado slices around the fish.

12. Cut the clingfilm-wrapped roll in half with a sharp knife on a chopping board. Using a moist towel, wipe the knife clean and cut each piece in half until you have eight. Remove the cling film before serving.

13. In the same manner, make three more rolls of dough.

14. Top the sushi roll with caviar, sesame seeds, and a spicy mayo sauce before serving.

EBI NIGIRI SUSHI

Ingredients

- 2 cups of sushi rice (short grain)
- 2 1/2 cups of water
- 1/4 cup of rice vinegar
- 1 tsp salt
- 2 tsp sugar
- Boiled shrimps

Instructions

1. Drain the water from the rice and rinse it thoroughly. In a rice cooker, combine 2 1/2 cups water with the sushi rice and cook according to package directions. Toss the rice with the vinegar, salt, and sugar when it has done cooking. In a large bowl, stir together all the ingredients using a rice paddle. After the rice has cooled down, form the rice into ovals (using saran wrap to prevent sticking). Each rice ball should have a small amount of wasabi on it, and then some boiling shrimp should be placed on top.

EASY CHIRASHI-ZUSHI WITH EDAMAME

Ingredients

- 3 cups of (*180ml cup of) Japanese Short Grain Sushi Rice
- 1/2 Carrot *sliced, blanched in salted water.
- 1/2-1 Cucumber *thinly sliced, slightly salted.
- 40 g Dried Shiitake *cooked Sweet Soy Broth (Sugar 1 : Soy Sauce 2 : Mirin 1)
- 1 cup of Edamame *cooked, removed from pods.
- Snow Peas
- 4 Eggs
- 1 tsp Oil
- Sushi Vinegar Ingredients
- 72 ml Japanese Rice Vinegar
- 60 g Sugar *slightly less 1/4 cup of
- 1 & 1/4 tsp Salt

Instructions

1. To obtain a firmer texture, cook rice with a little less water. After the rice has finished cooking, allow it to steam for ten minutes.
2. Sushi Vinegar is made by combining rice vinegar with sugar and salt to form a syrupy mixture. A big mixing bowl will need to be used to distribute the mixture.
3. Fans or cardboard can be used to assist the rice cool down more rapidly while it is being mixed. Rice with a quick cooling process has a glossy appearance.
4. After the rice has done cooking, allow it to steam for ten minutes.
5. Prepare the rest of the ingredients for combining and sprinkling on top before continuing.
6. Add salt to a bowl of thinly sliced cucumber and massage it for a few minutes before letting it sit for a while. Remove the Cucumber's extra water by squeezing it.

7. Slice the Dried Shiitake into thin strips after soaking them in cold water. (Or use Dried Shiitake that has already been sliced.) Pour the ingredients into a saucepan, add just enough water to cover, and simmer for 20 minutes or until the broth has thickened. Remove the surplus liquid by squeezing the mixture gently.
8. Cook the eggs in a tiny quantity of oil until they are hard and dry, then remove from the pan. Put it on a serving dish.
9. Blanching carrots and snow peas in salted water is a must. Be careful not to overcook the food.
10. Toss the sushi rice with the cucumber, edamame, and shiitake mushrooms.
11. Step 10 of the easy Chirashi-sushi with Edamame recipe
12. Toppings are the last touch

EASY AVOCADO EGG ROLLS

Prep Time: 5 m Cook Time: 5 m. Total Time: 10 m

Ingredients

- 3 avocados halved, peeled, and seeded.
- 1/2 cup of tomatoes diced.
- 1/3 cup of diced onion
- 2 tbsp chopped fresh cilantro leaves.
- salt and black pepper as need
- Juice of 1 lime
- 12 egg roll wrappers
- 1 cup of vegetable oil for frying
- For the cilantro dipping sauce
- 1/2 cup of fresh cilantro leaves loosely packed.
- 1/4 cup of sour cream
- 1 tbsp mayonnaise
- 1 jalapeno seeded and deveined.
- Juice of 1 lime
- 1 clove garlic
- Salt and freshly ground black pepper as need.

Instructions

1. Add salt and pepper to taste if necessary to food processor bowl of cilantro dipping sauce, process until smooth. Serve with chips. Set away for later.
2. In a large pan or Dutch oven, heat the vegetable oil.
3. In a medium bowl, gently mash avocados. Add salt, pepper, chopped onions, tomatoes, and lime juice.
4. Fill each wrapper with the avocado mixture one at a time. Wrap the filling in the bottom of the wrapper, tucking in the sides as you go. Keep rolling until you reach the very top of the wrapper. The edges of the wrapper should be rubbed with water and pressed to seal. When you're through, repeat with the rest of the wrappers.
5. Gently lay the egg rolls in the oil in batches and cook for 2 to 3 minutes, or until golden and crispy on both sides. Wrap in paper towels and place on a serving platter.
6. Serve with dipping sauce right away.
7. Enjoy!

INSIDE-OUT CHICKEN AVOCADO ROLLS

Prep Time: 5 m Cook Time: 5 m. Total Time: 10 m

Ingredients

- 1 cup of sushi rice
- 1/4 cup of sushi seasoning (see note)
- 2 nori sheets, halved.
- 1 tbsp sesame seeds, toasted.
- 1 tbsp black sesame seeds, toasted.
- 1 tbsp wasabi paste.
- 1 cup of shredded barbecued chicken
- 1 small avocado, cut into strips.
- 1 large red capsicum, cut into strips.

Instructions

1. Rinse and drain the rice three times or until the water is clear. In a sieve, put the rice. Afterwards, let it sit for 10 minutes.

2. Place 1 cup of water and 1 cup of rice in a pot and bring to a boil. Bring the water to a boil, then cover and simmer. Low heat is best. Cook for 12 minutes or until the rice has done soaking up the water. Removing the food from the heat is necessary. For ten minutes, remain seated with your head covered. A big ceramic dish should be used for this. Break up any lumps by using a plastic spatula to stir the rice. Adding spice gradually while raising and rotating rice to near-coldness can help the rice retain its texture.

3. Make sushi by placing a piece of nori on the sushi mat and pressing it down. Spread a quarter of the rice on the nori using wet fingertips. Mix sesame seeds together. Toss rice with a quarter of the sesame mixture.

4. Wrap the rice with plastic. To face up the nori, flip the mat. Slide the nori-side of the plastic onto the mat. Apply a small amount of wasabi paste to the nori's center. On top of the wasabi, place a quarter of the chicken, avocado, and capsicum. Using a mat, tightly roll the dough into a roll. Carefully remove mat from plastic wrapper.

5. To make eight pieces, slice the roll in half. Remove and dispose of any plastic. Use the remaining ingredients to make 32 pieces of candy. Serve.

SMOKED SALMON AND AVOCADO SUSHI

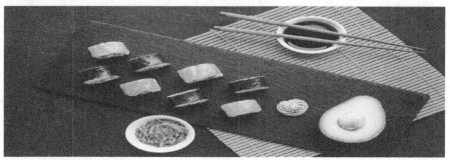

40m prep 15m cook.

Ingredients

- 430g (2 cups of) kochukaru rice, rinsed, drained.
- 750ml (3 cups of) cold water
- 125ml (1/2 cup of) rice vinegar
- 2 tbsp caster sugar
- 1/2 tsp salt
- 6 nori sheets
- 1 1/2 tbsp good-quality whole-egg mayonnaise
- 1/2 tsp wasabi paste.
- 200g sliced smoked salmon.
- 1 avocado, halved, stone removed, peeled, thinly sliced.
- 125ml (1/2 cup of) light soy sauce
- 2 tbsp mirin

Instructions

1. Rice and water
2. Do you have any questions about how much you'll need?
3. The quantity of each component may be found by clicking on the underlined text. There's no need to keep reversing pages!
4. a pot of water and some salt. Bring to a boil over high heat by covering the pot with a lid. The water should be absorbed in 12 minutes at a low temperature. Removing the food from the heat is necessary. To cool down a bit, place the covered dish in the refrigerator for 10 minutes (see microwave tip).
5. In a small container, combine vinegar, sugar, and salt. Add rice to a bowl of your choice, such as a glass or ceramic one. Break up any lumps with a wooden spoon or rice paddle. Gently incorporate the vinegar mixture into the rice, making sure that the rice doesn't become too moist. Until the rice has cooled, keep folding and fanning it (this should take about 15 minutes).

6. Clean your sushi mat and lay it out horizontally on the counter. A nori sheet should be placed 2cm from the edge closest to you, shiny side down. Wet your hands and distribute 3/4 cup of rice over the nori sheet, leaving a 3cm-wide border at the edge closest to you.

7. Combine the mayonnaise and wasabi in a small bowl and stir to combine well. A small amount of the wasabi mixture should be spread over the rice in the middle. Top with two salmon fillets and a few slices of avocado. Pick up the edge of the mat that is closest to your face. While rolling the mat to encompass the rice and nori, keep the filling in place. Five additional rolls may be made by using the remaining nori, rice, and filling.

8. The soy sauce and mirin should be mixed in a small serving dish before serving. Take a sushi roll and slice it into 2cm-thick pieces. Serve with mirin sauce on a plate.

TAMAGO SUSHI RECIPE

Prep Time: 15 minutes Cook Time: 45 minutes. Total Time: 1 hour

Ingredients

- 1 cup of sushi rice (uncooked short-grain sushi rice)
- 1 cup of water
- 1 ½ tbsp optional sushi vinegar (or mixing 1 tbsp rice vinegar, 1/2 tbsp sugar)
- 4 eggs
- 2 tbsp water
- 1/4 tsp rice vinegar
- 1 ½ tbsp sugar
- 1 tbsp mirin
- 1/4 tsp salt
- oil
- nori
- optional soy sauce for serving.

Instructions

1. Prepare Rice for Sushi
2. Rice and water should be washed and added to the rice cooker at the same time. Once the food has cooled down, take it to a big bowl. Stir in the sushi vinegar while the mixture is still extremely hot (or the mixture of rice vinegar, sugar, and salt).
3. Prepare Sushi with Tamagoyaki (fried rice balls).
4. In a separate dish, whisk the eggs until they are light and fluffy. Do not overbeat the eggs when making the omelet.
5. Stir together water, rice vinegar, sugar, and mirin in a separate basin until the sugar is completely dissolved. Set aside.
6. spice mixture to the egg mix. Whisk with care. Filter the egg mixture in a sieve to remove any grit. Preferably, put the mixture in a pourable measuring cup or can for ease of use in the kitchen.
7. Make sure the pan is heated to medium-high before you begin cooking the tamagoyaki. A folded paper towel can be used to coat the pan with oil.
8. Pour a thin layer of the seasoned egg mixture into the pan once the oil is heated. Allow the liquid to reach the pan's edge by

tilting the pan.

9. Roll the egg into a log shape once it's set but still a little soft on the surface. If you overcook the egg, it will not adhere to the log when you roll it. (It doesn't matter if your eggs aren't folded perfectly).

10. Remove the rolled omelets from the pan and use a paper towel to add extra oil. Apply the oil to the bottom of the omelets before placing it in the pan.

11. Cover the bottom of the pan with another layer of egg mixture. The mixture should be able to flow underneath the omelets by lifting it.

12. Start rolling the log back onto the set egg as soon as this new layer has set somewhat and is still soft on the top.

13. Continue until all the egg mixture has been utilized.

14. Take the tamagoyaki out of the pan and set it on a sushi mat. Shape the tamagoyaki while it is still hot, after you've wrapped it. Allow it to sit for about five minutes before using it again.

15. Set aside the tamagoyaki once it has been sliced into 12 equal pieces.

Prepare Tamayo Sushi.

16. Use a pair of scissors to cut the nori seaweed into 1/8-inch-long strips. Set away for later.

17. Shape a long, oval-shaped mound of cooked rice (approximately 1 12 inches in diameter) using 3/4 of a fistful. Gently flatten the bottom by squeezing the rice. (To avoid stickiness, soak your hands in vinegar water**.)

18. Put a slice of tamagoyaki on top of the rice and push down hard.

19. To keep the tamagoyaki in place on the rice, use a nori strip to wrap it around the whole width of the sushi. Make a total of 12 pieces by repeating the process.

20. The tam ago sushi is ready to be served. Soy sauce can be served as an optional condiment.

JAPANESE MISO EGGPLANT

Prep Time 10 m Cook Time 30 minutes. Total Time 40 m

Ingredients

- 1 ½ pounds Japanese eggplant (about 5 eggplants)
- 1 tbsp vegetable oil, canola oil, or grapeseed oil
- ⅓ cup of white or yellow miso paste
- 1 tbsp minced fresh ginger.
- 1 tbsp mirin or sake (optional; see note)
- 1 tsp toasted sesame oil
- 1 tsp rice or white wine vinegar
- Freshly ground pepper as need
- 2 tbsp sesame seeds
- Scallions, white and green sections, thinly cut for garnish.

Instructions

1. Prepare a 400°F oven. Aluminum foil or parchment paper can be used to line a rimmed baking pan. Cut the eggplant in half along its long axis, creating two long, flat pieces.

2. It is best to bake the eggplant with its sliced side up. Coat the sliced sides of the eggplant with a thin layer of oil. About 25 minutes in the oven should do the trick; the eggplant should be extremely soft and slightly browned on the top. The eggplant should be removed, and the oven temperature should be adjusted to broil.

3. Stir in a small bowl the miso, ginger, and sesame oil as well as the vinegar and pepper. Brush the roasted eggplant with the mixture, being sure to cover the entire surface with it. Sesame seeds can be sprinkled on top. Bake for another 4 minutes, until the tops are toasted, and the sesame seeds begin to brown. Be cautious not to overcook them, as they may burn.

4. Immediately after removing from the oven, sprinkle the scallions on top (which I forgot to do for these photos). Serve hot or warm.

SPICY EGGPLANT SUSHI

Prep Time 15 m Cook Time 30 minutes. Total Time 45 minutes

Ingredients

For the Rice

- ⅔ cup of sushi rice
- ¾ cup of + 2 tbsp. water
- ½ tbsp. salt
- ½ tbsp. rice vinegar

For the Filling

- 2 tbsp. vegetable oil
- 1 garlic clove minced.
- 2 tbsp. Asian chili paste.
- 1 scallion
- ½ medium eggplant sliced into thin strips

For Finishing and Serving

- 2 nori sheets
- sesame seeds
- soy sauce or tamari
- wasabi
- pickled ginger

Instructions

1. Rice is ready.
2. Using a sieve, pour the rice into the flowing water and let it soak for 1-2 minutes.
3. Add the rice and other ingredients to a small saucepan and bring to a boil. Place a lid on the pan and simmer for about 20 minutes or until the liquid has been absorbed completely.
4. Take it out of the oven and leave it covered for another 10 minutes before serving.
5. The Eggplant should be boiled.
6. Put oil in a medium-sized pan and heat it on a medium-low flame. When you're done, add some chili paste, garlic cloves, and salt. About a minute and a half.
7. In a single layer, place the eggplant slices. Cook for about 5 minutes on each side, or until the meat is fork-tender and browned.
8. Sushi is rolled.
9. Using a pair of scissors, snip off approximately a third of the nori sheet's length.
10. Bamboo mats may be used to place one of

your sheets on.

11. Keep a small dish of water nearby in case you need to rehydrate. Wet your hands and spread a thin coating of rice over the nori.

12. To assemble, place half of the eggplant in a single row down the nori's width, roughly an inch apart from one another. Slice half of your onion stalks and place them next to your eggplant.

13. Closely roll the bamboo mat and the end of the nori over your filling. Continue rolling by tucking the end of the nori into the roll and pressing it firmly against the mat.

14. Slice into eight pieces once the dough has been flattened out. Repeat this process with the remaining rice and filling on your second nori sheet.

15. Soy sauce or tamari, wasabi, and pickled ginger can be added to the sesame seeds before serving.

OTORO SUSHI TWO WAYS

PREP TIME:10 mins TOTAL TIME:10 mins

Ingredients

- sushi-grade odor (fatty tuna)
- sushi rice pillows
- yuzu
- For Serving
- soy sauce
- wasabi
- sushi ginger

Instructions

1. Trim the edges of the piece after removing the skin.
2. Slice to your preferred thickness. A thinner slice is advised because of the high fat content.
3. Remove the meat from the skin by slicing it. To prepare negator donburi, you'll need to use this section of the tuna, which is regarded one of the most delectable.
4. Using a kitchen flame, sear the Otero to bring out the umami qualities that have been hiding in the meat.
5. sushi pillows on top of each other Top the seared Otero with a squirt of yuzu juice. In addition to sushi ginger and soy sauce, garnish with a few slices of wasabi.
6. Closely roll the bamboo mat and the end of the nori over your filling. Continue rolling by tucking the end of the nori into the roll and pressing it firmly against the mat.
7. Slice into eight pieces once the dough has been flattened out. Repeat this process with the remaining rice and filling on your second nori sheet.
8. Soy sauce or tamari, wasabi, and pickled ginger can be added to the sesame seeds before serving.

IMITATION CRAB CALIFORNIA ROLL BURRITO

Prep Time40 minutes Cook Time0 minutes. Total Time40 minutes

Ingredients

- 2 cups of sushi
- 2 cups of water, +extra for rinsing rice
- 2 tbsp rice vinegar
- 2 tbsp sugar
- 1 tbsp kosher salt
- 16 ounces imitation crab meat
- 1/4 cup of mayonnaise
- 4 sheets nori
- 1 cucumber
- 2 carrots
- 1 cup of napa cabbage or regular cabbage
- 1 avocado
- 1 tsp sesame seeds

Instructions

1. Use cold water to repeatedly rinse the rice until the water runs clear. If you miss this stage, it won't get as sticky.
2. After adding 2 cups of water to a pot and bringing it to a boil, remove it from the heat.
3. It should be covered and simmered for 15 minutes at a lower temperature once it reaches a boil.
4. Cover the dish and let it sit for 10 minutes after taking it from the heat. There is no need to look at it.
5. Stir together brown sugar and salt in a microwave-safe container and cook for 30 to 45 seconds at high.
6. Fold the rice into the vinegar mixture to incorporate. Make sure the rice isn't too soft.
7. Wait for it to cool completely before moving on to the next step.
8. In a small food processor, combine imitation crab meat and mayonnaise and pulse until the mixture is finely chopped and well mixed.
9. You may also finely chop everything and then stir in the mayonnaise.

10. Slice the carrots, napa cabbage, and cucumber into thin strips (peel and remove the seeds of the cucumber first)
11. Thinly slice the avocado.
12. Layout a sheet of nori and one cup of rice on top of it. Then, using a spatula, spread the rice out to the very edge of the nori. Sesame seeds can be sprinkled on top of the dish for added flavor.
13. For the vegetables, use around 12 cups of julienned vegetables (you'll need to eyeball the amounts for the cabbage, carrots, and cucumber because you won't have a measuring cup big enough for those).
14. A quarter of an avocado should be placed along the side of the vegetables in a fanning pattern.
15. Stack a quarter of the crab mixture on top and form into a log.
16. Using the parchment paper, roll the nori into a compact log with the edges just touching by 14 - 12 inch.
17. The bottom of the burrito is made by folding the parchment in half and rolling the remaining paper tightly.
18. It's time to split the burrito in half.

SALTA LA-MAKI ROLL

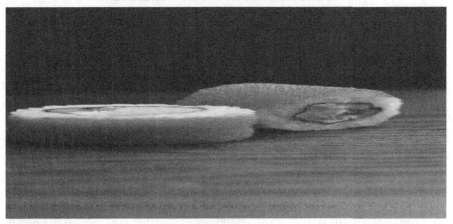

PREP TIME:10 mins TOTAL TIME:10 mins

Ingredients

- Potato Chips
- Cooked Sushi Rice
- Raw Salmon
- Roasted Zucchini
- Sriracha
- Soy Sauce

Instructions

1. Crunch up the potato chips, then spread a thin layer of sushi rice on top of them to form these rolls. Salmon and zucchini are rolled up with potato chips on the exterior, making a filling sandwich. Serve it with sriracha and soy sauce by slicing it in half and serving it on a plate. The chips should be consumed promptly so that they don't become mushy and lose their crispiness. (Within 30 minutes)

CRAB, AVOCADO AND MANGO ROLL

Prep: 2 min Cook: 25 min

Ingredients

- one pound lump crabmeat, drained and patted dry with paper towels.
- 1/4 cup of mayonnaise
- 4 tsp lemon juice
- 4 tsp light brown sugar
- 5 cups of cooked Sushi Rice, recipe follows.
- 4 toasted nori sheets
- 1 avocado, seeded, peeled.
- 1 mango, peeled.
- 1/2 red bell pepper, cored, seeded.
- 1/4 cup of black sesame seeds
- 2 cups of short-grain sushi rice
- 2 1/2 cups of water
- 1/4 cup of seasoned rice vinegar

Instructions

1. A bamboo sushi mat is a must-have piece of equipment while making sushi.
2. Wasabi, ginger, and soy sauce are some of the best accompaniments for this dish.
3. Using a medium-sized mixing bowl, combine the mayonnaise, lemon juice, and sugar with the crab meat.
4. The sushi mat should be covered with plastic wrap. Make a rectangle slightly smaller than the sushi mat by spreading 1 1/4 cups of rice on the plastic wrap with your damp fingertips. Cover the rice with nori. The crab combination should be arranged in the middle of the nori, leaving a 2-inch border at the top. Mix in a quarter of each of the mango and red bell pepper pieces before adding them to your crab mixture. Fold the rice over the filling and roll into a cylinder using the sushi mat as a guide. Remove the plastic film. Repeat with the rest of the ingredients. " Sprinkle the black sesame seeds on each roll.
5. Slice each cylinder into six pieces with a sharp, damp knife before serving (re-wet the knife after each slice). Serve the crab rolls with wasabi, sweet, pickled ginger, and soy sauce on a serving plate.

6. It's called sushi rice:
7. Can be found at Asian marketplaces with a focus on Asian products.
8. In a medium saucepan, bring the rice and water to a boil. In a pot, combine all ingredients and bring to a boil. Reduce the heat to low and cover the pan. 25 minutes of simmering time is required. With a fork, combine the rice and vinegar. Bake the rice on a baking sheet lined with parchment paper when it has finished cooking. Before using, allow the rice to cool fully.
9. 1/4 cup of seasoned rice vinegar

CRAB, AVOCADO AND MANGO ROLL

Prep: 2 min Cook: 25 min

Ingredients

- one pound lump crabmeat, drained and patted dry with paper towels.
- 1/4 cup of mayonnaise
- 4 tsp lemon juice
- 4 tsp light brown sugar
- 5 cups of cooked Sushi Rice, recipe follows.
- 4 toasted nori sheets
- 1 avocado, seeded, peeled.
- 1 mango, peeled.
- 1/2 red bell pepper, cored, seeded.
- 1/4 cup of black sesame seeds
- 2 cups of short-grain sushi rice
- 2 1/2 cups of water
- 1/4 cup of seasoned rice vinegar

Instructions

1. A bamboo sushi mat is a must-have piece of equipment while making sushi.
2. Wasabi, ginger, and soy sauce are some of the best accompaniments for this dish.
3. Using a medium-sized mixing bowl, combine the mayonnaise, lemon juice, and sugar with the crab meat.
4. The sushi mat should be covered with plastic wrap. Make a rectangle slightly smaller than the sushi mat by spreading 1 1/4 cups of rice on the plastic wrap with your damp fingertips. Cover the rice with nori. The crab combination should be arranged in the middle of the nori, leaving a 2-inch border at the top. Mix in a quarter of each of the mango and red bell pepper pieces before adding them to your crab mixture. Fold the rice over the filling and roll into a cylinder using the sushi mat as a guide. Remove the plastic film. Repeat with the rest of the ingredients. " Sprinkle the black sesame seeds on each roll.
5. Slice each cylinder into six pieces with a sharp, damp knife before serving (re-wet the knife after each slice). Serve the crab rolls with wasabi, sweet, pickled ginger, and soy sauce on a serving plate.

6. It's called sushi rice:
7. Can be found at Asian marketplaces with a focus on Asian products.
8. In a medium saucepan, bring the rice and water to a boil. In a pot, combine all ingredients and bring to a boil. Reduce the heat to low and cover the pan. 25 minutes of simmering time is required. With a fork, combine the rice and vinegar. Bake the rice on a baking sheet lined with parchment paper when it has finished cooking. Before using, allow the rice to cool fully.
9. 1/4 cup of seasoned rice vinegar

INARI SUSHI: RICE STUFFED TOFU POCKETS

Prep:30 mins Cook:60 mins Assemble:10 mins

Ingredients

- 2 cups of sushi rice, or medium-grain rice
- 2 tsp granulated sugar
- 2 tbsp rice vinegar
- 2 sheets nori, or gym, crumbled.
- 10 square inari pockets, cut in half.

Instructions

1. Sushi Rice should be prepared.
2. Organize the components.
3. A rice cooker or a saucepan on the stove can be used to make sushi rice.
4. Once the rice is cooked, use a spoon to fluff it up.
5. Allow to sit for a further 10 to 15 minutes with the lid on.
6. The vinegar and sugar should be whisked together in a bowl.
7. Large salad or wooden bowls work well for this. The rice should be spread out in a thin layer so that it cools down quickly.
8. When the rice is cold enough to handle, add the vinegar-sugar mixture and stir to combine. You may use a hand fan or magazine to speed up the cooling process. As you combine, keep fanning out.
9. Put the Inari Sushi together.
10. Mix the rice with the seaweed crumbles and seasonings.
11. Soak your hands with rice vinegar before handling the rice. It's up to you whether you weigh the rice and divide it into 20 equal parts or simply eyeball 20 zeppelin-shaped balls.
12. Ovals should be pressed firmly into the inari pockets to seal them in. Continue until you've used up all of the rice and pockets in your bag. Serve at once.
13. Enjoy.
14. inari pockets to seal them in. Continue until you've used up all of the rice and pockets in your bag. Serve at once.
15. 13. Enjoy.

HOMEMADE SUSHI ROLL RECIPE

PREP TIME: 10 mins COOK TIME: 15 mins. TOTAL TIME: 25 mins

Ingredients

- 1½ cup of Sushi rice
- 2 cups of Water
- 6 tbsp Sushi seasoning or rice wine vinegar
- 5 Nori sheets
- 100 g Chicken schnitzel or ready to eat tuna cans.
- 100 g Mayonnaise

Instructions

1. Using either a rice cooker or a regular pot, cook the sushi rice by adding rice and water together (Cook sushi rice according to packet instructions)
2. Add sushi seasoning to the rice once it's cooked, and then gently toss it all together.
3. Lay down a flat tray with the sushi rice and allow it to cool to room temperature.
4. To keep your hands and knives from becoming stuck in the sticky rice, you'll want to have a basin of water nearby.
5. Chopping board with nori sheet placed on top of rice when it has cooled down.
6. The nori sheet should be topped with a layer of sushi rice and flattened with your fingertips.
7. The center of the page is where you should place your fillings.
8. Close your fists and tuck them in. Seal the roll by drizzling a little water on the end of the nori sheet.
9. A sharp knife is used to chop the meat into equal halves. When your knife gets too sticky, put it in the water and let it soak for a few minutes.
10. Pickled ginger and soy sauce are great accompaniments to this dish.

SALMON & CUCUMBER SUSHI ROLLS

Prep:20 mins Cook:20 mins

Ingredients

- 2 nori sheets
- 100g skinless salmon fillet (use fresh), thinly sliced lengthways.
- ¼ cucumber, deseeded, thinly sliced lengthways
- squeeze wasabi, +extra to serve.
- pickled sushi ginger, to serve.
- light soy sauce, to serve
- salmon roe, to serve (optional)
- For the rice
- 100g sushi rice
- 2 tsp sake or mirin (optional)
- 1 tbsp caster sugar (omit if using mirin)
- 25ml rice vinegar

Instructions

1. Make the rice first. Using a colander and your hands, rinse the sushi rice until it is completely clear. Allow 15 minutes of draining time.

2. Add 200ml of water and the sake or mirin, if using, to a pot and bring to a boil. Bring to a boil, then reduce to a low heat, cover, and cook for 20 minutes. It is vital to remove the meal from the heat. Cover and let aside for 15 to 20 minutes.

3. Fill a big bowl with the mixture and set aside. Pour the vinegar and a generous amount of salt over the rice and stir to combine. If using, dissolve the sugar in the vinegar mixture. Wait until you're ready to use it by covering it with a moist tea towel and storing it at room temperature.

4. It's best to put half the rice on a nori sheet before placing it on a bamboo mat. With the salmon and cucumber, you should be cautious not to overfill the rice. Dab some wasabi on the outside of the filling with your finger.

5. When you've reached the end, securely roll the package and squeeze to close it. Add more wasabi and repeat with the rest of the nori mixture, salmon, and cucumbers. Serve with more wasabi, ginger, soy sauce, and salmon roe, if desired, on each roll. One day in the fridge is all it takes.

FRUIT SUSHI

Ingredients

- 1 1/2 cup of sushi rice
- 2 cups of water
- 3 tbsp sugar
- 1/4 tsp salt
- 1 cup of coconut milk
- 1 1/2 tsp vanilla extract
- Fruit (any fruit will do, such as pineapple, kiwi, mango, banana, strawberry, etc.)

Instructions

1. Rinse the rice well under running water. Drain and rinse the rice before adding it to a large bowl with water. Rinse the rice with your hands until the water becomes milky white. Remove the water using a sieve.
2. Cook rice. To make a risotto, add the water, rice, salt, sugar, and bring to a boil. Cook the rice for a further 12-15 minutes at a lower temperature.
3. Add a splash of coconut milk to the mix. To finish the rice, add some coconut milk once it's been given a chance to absorb the water.
4. Before serving, let the rice to cool. After it's done cooking in the pot, put the rice to a lined tray to cool down.
5. Fruits should be cut. Just as with sushi fillings, chop the fruit into long sticks.
6. Use plastic wrap to spread rice. Using your hands or a spoon, form a rectangle shape out of part of the rice.
7. Fruit slices should be arranged. The strips of fruit should be placed around two-thirds of the way from the beginning of the rice.
8. Roll out the sushi. A log-like structure should be formed once you have added all the appropriate fruits. Make sure the sushi doesn't unravel.
9. To be of service. Sliced cantaloupe serves as pickled ginger and fresh fruit purée serves as soy sauce for the sushi rolls. Eat with chopsticks, of course!

MARINATED FRESH TUNA NIGIRI SUSHI

Ingredients

- 1 slice Sashimi grade maguro (lean tuna)
- 1 Sushi Rice
- The marinating sauce.
- 2 tbsp each Soy sauce and sake
- 1 tbsp Mirin
- 1 Green onions
- 1 Wasabi

Instructions

1. The marinating sauce is made by combining the soy sauce, sake, mirin, and green onions. To make nigiri sushi, cut the tuna into the right size pieces Marinate the tuna slices in the sauce for about 30 minutes in the refrigerator before serving them.

2. Squeeze sushi rice into spherical shapes using your hands. Wasabi should be sprinkled on top, followed by the tuna that has been marinated. Done!

CHICKEN TEMPURA ROLLS

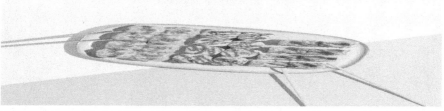

1 hours

Ingredients

- 2 cups of sushi rice
- 1/2 cup of rice vinegar
- 1/4 cup of sugar
- 1 tsp salt
- 1/2-pound frozen breaded chicken tenders
- 2/3 cup of thawed orange juice concentrate
- 2 tbsp reduced-sodium soy sauce.
- 1 tsp minced fresh ginger root.
- 1/2 tsp crushed red pepper flakes.
- 1/2 tsp sesame oil
- Bamboo sushi mat
- 1-1/2 cups of sliced almonds chopped and toasted.
- 3 green onions (green portion only)
- 1 small sweet red pepper, julienned.
- 1 large navel orange, peeled, sectioned, and cut into thin strips.

Instructions

1. A big bowl with a lid should be used to rinse rice numerous times in a row until the water is clear. Add 2 cups of water to the big pot with the prepared vegetables. Allow to sit for 30 minutes.

2. Cover the saucepan and cook it to a rolling boil over high heat. Cook for 13 minutes, or until all the water has been absorbed and the rice is soft, on low heat. Taking the food from the heat is necessary. Allow to stand for 10 minutes, covered.

3. Mix vinegar, sugar, and salt in a small bowl and whisk until the sugar is dissolved.

4. In a shallow bowl, add one cup of the vinegar mixture, then the rice. The remaining vinegar mixture should be set aside for assembling. Stir the rice until it has reached room temperature using a wooden paddle or spoon. Keep wet by covering with a damp towel. You may prepare the rice combination up to 6 hours ahead of time and keep it covered with a moist towel at room temperature. Refrigeration is not required.)

5. To chill the chicken, bake it according to the instructions on the package. Make long, thin strips out of it. Set aside 1/2 cup of the mixture for serving in a large dish with

the juice concentrate, soy sauce and ginger. Chicken is ready to be served when it is tossed with the remainder of the orange mixture.

6. Wrap a sushi mat with plastic wrap to protect it. Spread 1/4 cup of almonds evenly on a piece of plastic wrap, forming a 9-in. x 6-in. square. Press the rice into an equal layer over the almonds with your hands, using the vinegar mixture to moisten your hands.

7. Chicken mixture, green onion, red pepper and orange strips should be arranged about 1-1/2 inches from the bottom of a rectangle. Rolled away from you on a bamboo mat, keep the rice filling inside the rectangle. Squeeze the roll into a compact log with the mat's support. Remove the mat and put the tempura roll away. Create six tempura rolls by doing this.

8. Make 1-1/2-inch slices out of each. Reserving some of the sauce, serve.

SHRIMP EGG ROLLS

PREP TIME:30 mins COOK TIME:15 mins. TOTAL TIME:45 mins

Ingredients

- ½ lb. shrimp
- 1 Tbsp's sake
- ⅛ tsp kosher or sea salt
- 1 knob ginger
- 1 Negi (long green onion)
- 5 egg roll (Haruaki) wrappers
- 4 Tbsp Negi miso
- ¾ cup of neutral-flavored oil (vegetable, rice bran, canola, etc.) (for deep frying)
- Flour mixture "glue"
- 1 tsp all-purpose flour (plain flour)
- 1 tsp water

Instructions

1. If the head is still connected, take it. Take the top layer. Using a skewer, devein the shrimp's backside. The vein travels down the back of the torso. The shrimp's head should be approximately 12 inches below the tip of the skewer when inserting it sideways. The vein will rise to the surface, allowing you to remove it with the skewer or your hand. The vein can be reinserted if it has been damaged. Don't stress if you can't locate the vein. [Recommended] The shrimp should be scrubbed in a dish with a little salt, 1 tablespoon of potato/corn starch, and 2 tablespoons of water until you see filthy liquid. Rinse until the water runs clear.

2. Slice diagonally across the tail's tip (as you see below).

3. The tail may be cleaned by squeezing the water out of the cut tip of the knife while holding it down on the tail and moving it from left to right. In the absence of this step, the oil may spatter because of the water in the tail.

4. All of the tail's translucent Ness has now spread to its entirety.

5. A pair of diagonal cuts should be made on the underside of the shrimp.

149

6. Straighten the shrimp as much as possible using your hands to get the correct form.
7. Put the shrimp, sake, and salt in a small basin and toss to combine. Make sure it's marinating until you're ready to use it.
8. Cut the ginger into julienned strips after peeling the skin.
9. Thinly slice the neigh by cutting it in half diagonally.
10. To split the egg rolls, cut the egg roll wrappers in half and take off one at a time.
11. In a bowl, combine flour and water and stir until a smooth paste forms. A tiny bowl of Negi Miso is all you need.
12. We're almost there.
13. The long side of an egg roll wrapper should be towards you, with one of the short sides facing away from you. On one side of the wrapper, place the Negi Miso and shrimp, with the tail sticking out about half of the way.
14. Ginger & Negi should be garnished with julienned ginger. Turn over the shrimp and fold the bottom edge of the wrapper over it.
15. Begin rolling after folding the side edge over to meet the shrimp.
16. Continue rolling until you reach the wrapper's end. Sprinkle the flour mixture on the wrappers outside border with a few tiny dabs. Wrap as many shrimps and wraps as possible.
17. To deep fry.
18. A medium saucepan or big frying pan with a depth of 12 inches of oil should be used. Place a chopstick tip in the heated oil and fry until it is hot and begins to boil.
19. Place the egg rolls one at a time in the pan., making sure they don't touch any other. Do not overcrowd. If you have one, use it. Cook until golden brown and cooked through. Each side will take about three minutes.
20. Pour any remaining oil onto a paper towel before removing from the pan. With Negi Miso.

FRIED TOFU INARIZUSHI

Prep:60 mins Cook:60 mins Total:2 hrs.

Ingredients

- 1 1/2 cups of Japanese rice
- 1 2/3 cups of water
- 3 tbsp rice vinegar
- 1 1/2 tbsp sugar
- 1/2 tsp salt
- 2 tbsp white sesame seeds
- For Cooking Aburaage
- 6 abura-age (deep-fried tofu, blanched)
- 1 cup of dashi soup stock
- 2 1/2 tbsp sugar
- 2 tbsp mirin
- 2 tbsp soy sauce

Instructions

1. How to Make French Fries from Scratch
2. Rinse the rice in a basin with cold water before cooking. Rinse until the water is nearly clear. Set a timer for 30 minutes and drain the rice in a colander.
3. Rice should be put in a rice cooker along with the appropriate amount of water. For at least 30 minutes, let the rice soak in the water. Turn on the stove.
4. Cook sugar and salt in rice vinegar in a pot to make sushi vinegar. Cook sugar in a small saucepan over low heat until it dissolves, about 5 to 10 minutes. Cool the vinegar mixture.
5. A big bowl or platter can be used to spread out the hot steamed rice. Using a shimeji (rice spatula), swiftly incorporate the rice in the vinegar mixture.
6. Toss sesame seeds onto sushi rice and enjoy Make sushi rice mounds using wet palms.
7. Cut aburaage in half so that each piece has an open-end while you are doing it.
8. Cook sugar, mirin, and soy sauce in a medium saucepan until the mixture comes to a boil, then take off the heat.
9. Pour in the aburaage and reduce the heat. Take the lid and simmer until the liquid is nearly gone. The temperature should be lowered.
10. Lightly press a piece of aburaage to remove any remaining liquid. Get out the pouch and fill it with sushi rice. Close the pouch by folding in the open end.

FRUIT SUSHI

Prep:60 mins Cook:60 mins Total:2 hrs.

Ingredients

- 1 roll berry fruit tape, cut into six smaller strips.
- 1 cup of uncooked jasmine white rice
- ¼ cup of granulated sugar
- ¼ cup of coconut milk
- ½ tsp almond extract
- 2 tbsp sweetened shredded coconut.
- 1 tsp honey, +additional for adhering rice
- ¼ tsp salt
- Kiwi sliced vertically.
- Red skinned peach, skin on, sliced vertically into strips.
- Strawberry thinly sliced.
- Maple syrup, for dipping

Instructions

1. Rice should be brought to a boil, then reduced to a simmer in a cup of water. Cover the rice and cook it until most of the water has been absorbed. Take the lid off and let it sit for 15 minutes before removing.

2. After removing the cover, add the salt and sugar to the mixture. Stirring regularly, cook for a further 20 minutes or until the sauce has thickened. Set the rice in the refrigerator for at least 30 minutes.

3. Form 2 tablespoons of rice into a tiny log using your palms. Wrap a slice of kiwi, strawberry, or peach with fruit tape and place it on top. If necessary, seal the ends of the fruit tape together with a drop of water.

FUTOMAKI - BIG SUSHI ROLL

Prep:60 mins Cook:60 mins Total:2 hrs.

Ingredients

- 3 sheets nori
- 15 -20 large shrimp, cooked.
- 3 imitation crab sticks
- 1/3 cup of carrot, finely grated.
- 1 small cucumber (preferably Lebanese or Japanese)
- 1 avocado
- 2 leaves romaine lettuce
- 4 cups of cooked rice, seasoned with sushi vinegar (see #315511 Easy Sushi Rice)
- 1/4 cup of rice vinegar

Instructions

1. Seaweed may be split in half lengthwise.
2. using scissors.
3. Make long, thin strips.
4. out of the cucumber using a mandolin or other sharp knife.
5. Cut the avocado into thin strips after removing the pit. Remove the lettuce's cent.
6. er ribs, then shred it.
7. Rinse a small bowl with water and add one tablespoon of rice vinegar.
8. to prevent the rice from sticking.
9. Roll up a bamboo rolling mat with plastic wrap around it. Place a piece of nori on the plastic wrap with the rough side up.
10. Spread half of the nori with a handful of rice, leaving one end unadorned "on the other side of the transparent nori. Repeat this process to cover the second half of the seaweed.
11. a row of 5-6 shrimp and space them approximately 2 inches apart "coming in from the shortest distance possible.
12. Seaweed sticks and shredded lettuce are added next.
13. To resemble logs of wood, stack avocado slices and shredded carrots on top of the shrimp. Each roll should be filled with one-third of the filling ingredients.
14. Gently roll up the mat, starting from the near side. Remove the mat from the roller. Make two more rolls by using the same process.
15. Eight slices from each roll. Soy sauce, wasabi, and pickled ginger are all good accompaniments.

10-MINUTE GAZPACHO

prep time: 10 MINUTES total time: 10 MINUTES

Ingredients

- 2 pounds fresh tomatoes
- 1 English cucumber, peeled.
- 1 small red bell pepper, cored.
- quarter of a red onion, peeled.
- 2 garlic cloves, peeled.
- 1/4 cup of lightly packed fresh basil leaves
- 2 tbsp fresh lemon juice
- 1 tbsp olive oil
- fresh-cracked black pepper
- Extra tomatoes, red onion, basil, olive oil, and/or salt and pepper are optional garnishes.

Instructions

1. Add all ingredients to a large food processor and pulse until smooth and creamy.
2. If required, s
3. Eason with more salt, pepper, and/or lemon juice, and then serve.
4. A few hours in the fridge will do the trick. Alternatively, you may serve it right away with your preferred garnishes

MATZAH PIZZA

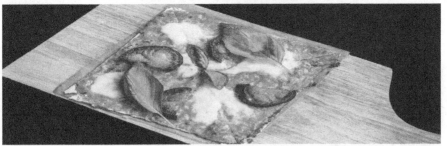

PREP TIME: 5 mins COOK TIME: 10 mins. TOTAL TIME :15 mins

Ingredients

- 1 piece matzah
- 1/8 cup of tomato sauce
- 1/4 cup of shredded mozzarella
- 1/8 tsp dried garlic
- 1/8 tsp dried oregano
- 5 slices fresh mozzarella or more shredded mozzarella
- Fresh basil

Instructions

1. Turn oven to 350 degrees and prepare a baking sheet lined with parchment paper.
2. Matzah can be topped with shredded cheese if desired. To set, bake for 2-3 minutes on a parchment-lined baking sheet.
3. Spread the sauce over the matzah. Garnish with oregano and garlic.
4. Fresh mozzarella or shredded mozzarella and basil should be sprinkled over the top.
5. Bake until the cheese has melted and reached a gooey consistency. Eat!

CHOCOLATE CHIP BANANA BARS

cook time: 15 MINUTES. total time: 25 MINUTES

Ingredients

- 4 bananas (mine weighed around 460g when peeled)
- 120g peanut butter (I use creamy peanut butter) - it can be smooth or crunchy.
- 250g gluten-free oats
- 125g chocolate chips

Instructions

1. Make sure your oven is preheated to 160C Fan / 180C degrees Fahrenheit. Tins of any shape and size can be used, although 8x8inch square tins are the most common. The smaller the tin, the tastier it will be.
2. Mash the bananas in a basin until they are smooth.
3. Add peanut butter to the mixture. Don't forget to thoroughly combine your peanut butter before adding it to the recipe, or even microwave it for a small period to soften it up.
4. Add the oats and blend well.
5. Your chocolate chips should make up about 105 grams of the mixture.
6. Spread the batter evenly into the tin, making sure it's evenly distributed.
7. Add the rest of the chocolate chips on the top of the brownies.
8. Allow 15 minutes in the oven.
9. Cut into bars when they have cooled. Enjoy!

GODZILLA ROLLS

Prep T: 10 minutes Cook Time: 3 minutes.Cook Time: 3 minutes.

Ingredients

- Sushi Rice
- 1 sheet Nori, dry roasted seaweed
- 3 pieces shrimp tempura prepared.
- 2 slices avocado
- 3 tsp cream cheese
- ½ cup of flour
- tempura batter
- oil for frying
- For the Spicy Mayo:
- ½ cup of mayonnaise
- 2 tbsp Sriracha sauce
- 1 dash sesame oil

Instructions

1. Using a cutting board, place the bamboo sushi rolling mat horizontally from you. Wrap the bamboo with plastic to protect it. Stack on a sheet of dried seaweed, shiny side down, on top of the mat. Using your hands, push sushi rice into the seaweed.

2. On a bamboo sushi mat, seaweed and rice are arranged.

3. The seaweed should be on top of the sushi layer. Lay a strip of seaweed over the shrimp tempura, avocado, and cream cheese. As the bamboo mat is rolled forward, the components in the sushi cylinder are pressed together (the KEY is to roll it TIGHT). Remove the rolled sushi by pressing hard on the bamboo mat with your hands. See the video below for further rolling training.

4. Fillings on nori for sushi

5. If you don't have a deep fryer, you may deep fry the rice roll in oil heated to 350 degrees for about 3 minutes or until the tempura batter is crispy and golden brown. Cooking the roll until golden brown on both sides requires just approximately 1/2 to 1 cup of oil in a frying pan. Cool for a few minutes before serving.

6. Rolls filled with tempura battered shrimp.

7. It is ideal to cut the sushi roll into four or five pieces using a very sharp knife. Add a dollop of spicy mayo.

8. Eaten with chopsticks, a shrimp tempura Godzilla roll looks like this:

9. For the Mayo with a Kick:

10. Mix mayo, sriracha, and sesame oil in a small bowl.

11. A dish with sriracha and sesame oil for the mayo-based dressing

12. Stir the mixture well. Make sure it's cold before using.

HAM & CHEESE CUCUMBER "SUSHI"

Prep Time: 10 m Cook Time: 3 minutes.Cook Time: 3 minutes.

Ingredients

- 1 cucumber
- 2 slices cheddar cheese
- 2 slices all-natural deli meat
- ⅓ cup of carrot (35 g)

Instructions

1. In big 1-inch (2 12 cm) thick slices, cut the cucumber into cubes.
2. A half-inch (1 cm) of cucumber should be left in the middle of the cucumber while hollowing it out.
3. Serve the deli meat in the form of a roll.
4. Fill the middle of the cucumbers with deli meat, cheese, and carrots.
5. Closely seal the container and keep it in the fridge.

MAKI WITH HAM AND VEGETABLES

Preparation: 1 hr. 20 min.

Ingredients

For the sushi rice
- 125 grams sushi rice
- 150 milliliters water
- 1 piece kombu seaweed (2x4 cm)
- 1 tbsp rice vinegar
- 1 sugar
- ½ splat

For the omelets
- 2eggs
- 1 tbsp mirin
- 1 sugar
- soy sauce
- salt
- 1 tbsp sesame oil
- For the carrots
- 2carrots
- 5 tbsp mirin
- 1 sugar
- 1 tbsp rice vinegar
- Salt

For the filling
- ¼cucumber
- 150 grams pickled daikon radish
- 150 grams cooked ham
- 2roasted nori seaweed
- vegetables (for garnish)

Instructions

1. Rinse the sushi rice before the water runs clear and then drain it well. Put rice and kombu in a saucepan and bring to a boil over medium heat. For two minutes, bring to a boil over high heat. Allow the rice to cook for about 10 minutes on low heat before taking from the pot. After 10 minutes of cooling, remove the rice from the heat, cover, and refrigerate. Another pot should be filled with vinegar and sugar and salt to be warmed.

2. Rinse and drain the rice. Remove the kombu and add the vinegar combination to the kombu and vinegar mixture and stir well. Stir the rice occasionally while it cools down.

3. Salt, sugar, and soy sauce are all you need for the omelet. Eggs and oil are heated in a nonstick pan, then the mixture is poured into the pan. Cook the omelet until it reaches a firm set in the middle. Using a serrated knife, slice the meat into thin strips.

4. Carrot matchsticks may be made by rinsing, peeling, and cutting the carrots. In a saucepan, combine them with the mirin, rice vinegar, and sugar. After 1 minute, remove from heat and allow it cool.

5. To make the filling, split the cucumber in half and remove the seeds. To prepare, thinly slice both the ham and the radishes.

6. To make the sushi, place a bamboo mat on top of half a nori sheet and distribute the sushi rice evenly, leaving a 1-2 cm border all the way around. Roll the omelet firmly after adding the vegetables, ham, and radish to the center. When cutting the roll, make sure the seam is pointing down. Serve the sushi with veggies on top of the platters.

KIMBAP (KOREAN SUSHI)

Prep:40 mins Cook:20 mins Total:1 hrCook Time: 3 minutes.

Ingredients

- 1 cup of uncooked glutinous white rice (sushi rice)
- 1 ½ cups of water
- 1 tbsp sesame oil
- salt, as need
- 2 eggs, beaten.
- 4 sheets sushi nori
- 1 cucumber
- 1 carrot
- 4 slices American processed cheese
- 4 slices cooked ham rips
- 2 tsp sesame oil

Instructions

1. In a sieve or colander, rinse the rice until the water runs clear. In a saucepan, mix the rice and water. Cook for 12-14 minutes, or until the rice is cooked, covered. Spread the rice out on a baking sheet and place it in the refrigerator to cool. To season the meal, all you need is salt and a tablespoon of sesame oil.

2. The eggs should be scrambled in a separate skillet while the rice is boiling. This will ensure a level layer of cooked egg when the rice has finished cooking. To cool the eggs, take them from the skillet and place them on a chopping board to rest for a few minutes.

3. Remove all but a half-inch of seaweed from the top of each nori sheet before dividing the cooled rice evenly between the two sheets. Layer the rice with strips of egg, cucumber, carrot, cheese, and ham. Use a bamboo sushi mat to roll each piece of nori into a cylindrical form from the bottom up. Brush each roll with half a teaspoon of sesame oil, then cut it into six equal pieces.

SUSHI RICE

prep Time: 5 M Cook Time: 15 MinutesCook Time: 15 Minutes

Ingredients

- 3 cups of sushi rice
- cups of water
- 0.5 cup of Rice vinegar
- 2 despite sugar
- 2 tsp fine salt

Instructions

1. To prepare the seasoning, heat the rice vinegar, sugar, and salt until thoroughly dissolved in a pot or microwave.
2. Sushi rice should be well rinsed before cooking in a heavy-bottomed pot (or rice cooker).
3. Once the rice is cooked, transfer it to a wooden or plastic container. There is no need to hide.
4. Evenly distribute the spice over the rice and chop it in with a wooden spoon.
5. Place rice near a window or use a fan to bring it to room temperature; never put rice in the refrigerator.

SPICY TUNA ROLLS

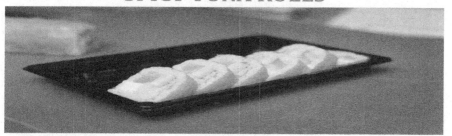

Prep Time: 25 Minutes Cook Time: 20 Minutes

Ingredients

- 1 tbsp mayonnaise
- 1 tsp spicy chilly sauce
- 1 tsp fresh lemon juice
- 1/2 tsp sesame oil

Instructions

1. To make the Spicy Sauce, combine all the ingredients in a small bowl.
2. Dish out the tuna as directed and cut it into small cubes.
3. Pour Spicy Sauce over tuna cubes and stir well.
4. Place 2 teaspoons of Spicy Tuna in the middle of a nori sheet covered with sushi rice.
5. Slices of avocado may be rolled up.
6. To serve, cut the sushi into six or eight pieces and garnish with soy sauce, wasabi, and cilantro.

CALIFORNIA ROLLS

Prep Time: 30 Minutes Cook Time: 15 Minutes

Ingredients

- 2/3 cup of sushi rice.
- 1 nori sheet
- 6 Surimi sticks (Imitation crab) – or crab meat
- 1/2 Avocado
- Variations may include:
- Black and/or white sesame seeds
- Masango (Capelin Roe)

Instructions

1. Wrap your bamboo mat with plastic wrap.
2. Cut a nori sheet in half using a knife.
3. Sprinkle a handful of sushi rice over the nori with a light touch.
4. Spread a tablespoon of MAs ago or sesame seeds equally over the top half of the rice using a spoon.
5. Flip the nori so that the rice is on the bottom of the bamboo mat.
6. Arrange the crab sticks at the end of the nori.
7. Place 1-2 thick avocado slices next to it.
8. Turn it inside out right now. Here are detailed instructions for rolling sushi inside out.
9. Cut the cake into 8 equal-sized pieces.
10. Wasabi, soy sauce, and pickled ginger are served on the side (gari).

Prep Time: 25 Minutes Cook Time: 20 Minutes

Ingredients	Instructions
## Ingredients	## Instructions

Ingredients

- 2 sheets of Nori
- 1⅓ cups of Sushi rice
- 150g King Prawns
- 100g Sushi Grade Salmon
- 100g Sushi Grade Tuna

Instructions

1. Cut a nori sheet into two halves. Layer one half of the bamboo mat on top of the other, rough side up. Keep the other half in a dry place for the next roll. Wet your hands and take a handful of rice from the rice container. Make a rice ball and lay it in the center of the nori sheet.

2. Distribute the rice evenly on the nori sheet. Rather of pushing the rice down, spread it out evenly. Reverse the nori with a fork and a downward-facing nori.

3. The following step is to prepare the filling for the rolls.

4. You've prepared your avocados and prawns. Brilliant! Let's get them all arranged. As you can see, I prefer very thick avocado slices. Prawns should be put "tail to tail" to avoid extra space between them during rolling.

5. If you've made it this far, it's reasonable to assume you've mastered the art of rolling sushi. If you're still not sure, take a look at the animated GIF below. In the spirit of full transparency, this approach is taken from a different recipe website (Spicy Tuna, to be precise).

6. Lift the sushi mat off the counter with your thumbs and fingers and roll the sushi. Open a flap in the mat and draw it tight from the ends toward the center, taking care not to push out the filling. Retighten the mat after pushing it forward so that the roll is rolled within the mat. Repeat the process a third time if required.

7. If you're still not sure, read our in-depth guide on making sushi.

8. The topping off is my favorite part of the procedure. Salmon and tuna should be sliced into broad, thin slices. My cutting isn't quite up to snuff, as you can see in the image below. A long fish knife might have been more efficient for this activity, but I'm using an ordinary kitchen knife.

9. After you've assembled the roll, place the slices on top of it. Do not try to overlap them by more than a half-centimeter (.6 inches).

10. It looks excellent, with a lot of large pieces! Then, pressing down on the mat, bind the fish to the rice. Make sure it's snug enough so the roll doesn't fall apart when you cut it in half. After pressing down on the rice, a second time, the exterior of your roll should look like the image above.

11. You're almost there. Now it's time to cut the roll into smaller pieces for easy serving. It's usually either 8 or 6. Everything is dependent on whether you intend to retain the end. That's how I usually work.

12. If you're having trouble, there is a technique to cut the roll without pulling it apart. Roll a strip of saran tape on top of the roll and cut through it with the rolling mat. That is usually a tremendous help....

13. Keep the knife wet and clean between each roll-cutting stroke as a rule of thumb. That is a tremendous help.

14. You may also top ikura with black sesame seeds, chopped green onions, or anything else that comes to mind. I'm sure slathering some teriyaki sauce on top wouldn't hurt.

15. If you liked this recipe and want to see more, please leave a remark. Please also share the news. Also, have a wonderful time.

HALLOWEEN CANDY SUSHI

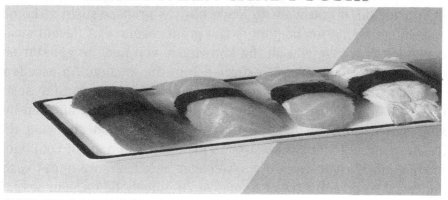

Prep Time: 30 mins Cook Time: 10 mins. Total Time: 40 mins

Ingredients

- 1 Tbsp. dairy-free butter
- 1 c. marshmallows
- 1 1/2 c. brown rice cereal
- 2 fruit roll-ups
- 12 gummy candies
- 1/4 c. chocolate sprinkles
- 1 Tbsp. green ball sprinkles

Instructions

1. Put butter in a medium pot and warm it slowly, stirring occasionally, until it is melted.

2. Once the marshmallows have melted, remove them from the heat and set them aside. Continually stir until the chocolate has completely melted and is smooth to the touch.

3. Then, using a wooden spoon, mix in the cereal until it is well covered. Before serving, allow the mixture to cool somewhat.

4. Baking pans should be lined with wax paper, not aluminum foil.

5. Spread 12 heaping tablespoons of the cereal marshmallow mixture on a baking sheet. Using cooking spray, coat your hands and form six balls into ovals and six into circles with a slightly indented center.

6. Wrap each "sushi" in a circle with a piece of fruit roll-up. Dip the edges of the oval forms in chocolate sprinkles to give them the appearance of black sesame seeds.

7. Gummy candies should be placed on top.

CONCLUSION

In conclusion, if you want to learn how to prepare sushi at home, a sushi cookbook for beginners is a great resource. A decent sushi cookbook may give you all the knowledge you need to get started, regardless of your level of experience in the kitchen. An excellent sushi cookbook will assist you in making tasty and genuine sushi dishes that will surprise your friends and family, from step-by-step instructions on making the rice to advise on choosing the freshest ingredients. So be sure to pick yourself a sushi cookbook for beginners right away if you're eager to learn more about sushi and want to give it a try at home. You'll quickly be on your way to mastering sushi with a little practice and the appropriate advice.

A sushi cookbook for beginners has several benefits, one of which is that it may demystify the sushi-making process. Sushi's novel ingredients and complex presentation might initially appear overwhelming. But, a good sushi cookbook may simplify the complicated sushi-making procedures into simple, understandable directions. Because of this, newcomers may find the procedure to be considerably less frightening and more approachable.

A sushi cookbook for beginners also has the added benefit of saving you money over time. In-restaurant sushi might be pricey, but with the help of a decent sushi cookbook, you can learn how to create your delectable sushi at home for a lot less money. Also, you'll feel proud knowing that you made it yourself!

Lastly, a beginner's sushi cookbook might be a fantastic opportunity to broaden your culinary horizons and try new things. Sushi is a distinctive and delectable food many people may not otherwise get to sample. You may expand your pallet and discover new tastes and textures by learning how to cook sushi at home.

Ultimately, anyone who wants to learn more about this interesting food will benefit from investing in a sushi cookbook for beginners. An excellent sushi cookbook may provide the direction and inspiration you need to start creating your delectable sushi meals at home, regardless of your level of experience in the kitchen.

Made in the USA
Las Vegas, NV
18 April 2024

88855068R00095